T0029069

PAVILION

First published in the UK in 2021 by
Pavilion Books Company Limited
43 Great Ormond Street
London
WC1N 3HZ

Text © Alice Haworth-Booth and Emily Haworth-Booth, 2021
Illustrations © Emily Haworth-Booth, 2021

The moral rights of the author and illustrator have been asserted

Publisher: Neil Dunnicliffe
Editors: Hattie Grylls and Martha Owen
Designer: Alice Haworth-Booth
Colour assistant: Rachel Stubbs

All rights reserved. No part of this publication may be reproduced, stored in a retrieval system, or transmitted in any form or by any means electronic, mechanical, photocopying, recording or otherwise, without prior permission of the copyright owner.

ISBN: 9781843654582

10 9 8 7 6 5 4 3 2 1

A CIP catalogue record for this book is available from the British Library

Reproduction by Mission, Hong Kong
Printed by 1010 Printing International Ltd, Singapore

This book can be ordered at www.pavilionbooks.com,
or try your local bookshop.

MIX
Paper from
responsible sources
FSC® C016973
FSC
www.fsc.org

PROTEST!

HOW PEOPLE HAVE COME TOGETHER TO CHANGE THE WORLD

By Alice & Emily Haworth-Booth

To our rebellious parents

CONTENTS

INTRODUCTION

The first big protest we remember going to was the march against the Iraq War in London in 2003. We weren't sure what to expect when we got there, and on the train we exchanged nervous smiles with other people holding placards. When we arrived we saw more people than we'd ever seen together in one place pouring out of the station. But it didn't take long for us to feel at home in the crowd. As the march set off, we took over the streets, singing and chanting together in a huge chorus. We were there to protest something sad, but the main feeling was one of love for humanity.

Because tens of millions of people took part in the protests all over the world, and because the war still happened, it made many people wonder if there was any point in protesting anymore. But marches are only ever part of a larger movement for change. There is no formula for a successful protest, no matter how many people agree with you, and success doesn't always match what's written on your placard.

The way protests work can be mysterious. Sometimes victory means building movements rather than achieving goals, and sometimes it's simply about sustaining hope and joy by coming together. Karl Marx saw revolution as a mole that is underground most of the time, making its way steadily forward, until suddenly it comes to the surface. Sometimes it seems like nothing is happening, but nevertheless, progress is being made. The march didn't stop the war, but it created a vibrant activist movement that was inclusive of difference and ready to challenge global governments on their harmful policies in the long term.

Since that first march we have discovered that protest can take almost any form. Dancing, sitting at lunch counters, taking your TV set out for a walk, growing vegetables, camping in the mountains, singing songs, sticking a loaf of bread on the end of a pole and carrying it around... all these things have changed the course of history. Protest is a creative art that is constantly reinventing itself. But at its heart is the idea of people coming together to speak the truth and change the world.

Many of history's most famous protests have an equally famous name attached to them. Figures like Martin Luther King, Jr. and Mahatma Gandhi have brought brilliant ideas and leadership to their movements, but they are individuals in what is most importantly a collective endeavour.

It is groups of people coming together to take action who are the real heroes of the stories in this book. It is their actions rather than their names that have entered the history books and changed the world, that have won breakthroughs in the struggle for civil rights, gay rights and trans rights, brought us things like votes for women and the eight hour working day, ended dictatorships and freed countries.

What happens next is up to you.

Alice & Emily Haworth-Booth, 2021

Note to reader

This book is not a complete history. It includes a selection of famous and less well-known movements, focusing on nonviolent protest. Rather than describe a handful of protests and their contexts in depth, we have chosen to present a broad range to give a sense of the many possibilities of what protest can be. And yet there is so much we have left out, because the history of protest is almost as big as the history of the world. Despite this, many movements have not been officially recorded in history, because it is not usually in the interests of the powerful to keep stories of resistance in the public memory.

We have written this book from the perspective of the protesters, and in line with our own sympathies. Protests have diverse aims, not all of which we agree with. Because we want this book to inspire readers, we have tried to choose examples where people are protesting for democracy and human rights and against oppression.

With some exceptions where movements overlap, or where it has felt more helpful to group things together in themes, we have told the story of protest chronologically. You can dip in and out or read it through from beginning to end, seeing how the influence of individual protests often unfolds across time, living on in future movements. The tactics sections at the end of each chapter collect together examples of particular ways to protest, like camping, theatre or making noise.

The experience of protest can be very different depending on where you are and how you are seen by the authorities. Although we have found lots of examples of people successfully finding creative ways to protest safely even when protests are banned, some of the stories in the book don't have happy endings, and many involve police or state violence. That is why it is so important to know your rights and understand that there are sometimes risks involved.

Experienced activists always do their research, prepare thoroughly and use a buddy system so their friends know where they are. If you are planning to protest, look up the laws in your country, take a friend or parent with you, and make sure you do what you need to do to stay safe.

Let's sit down

Protest in the Ancient World

THESE STONES ARE REALLY HEAVY

The First Workers' Strike, Ancient Egypt, 1170 BCE

Pharaoh Rameses III, the ruler of Egypt, wanted lots of pyramids to store all his gold to take to the afterlife. He had masses of jewellery and was terribly worried the pyramids wouldn't be finished before he died.

But the people building the pyramids had even bigger problems. The work was gruelling and they weren't getting enough food to eat. It was hot and dusty and the workers desperately needed things to change. They sat down and refused to work until they got their grain. It was a simple action that changed history.

The pyramid builders' sit-down protest is the earliest strike ever recorded. It was the first but certainly not the last time this effective tool would be used, proving that workers can be more powerful than their bosses when they collectively refuse to do their jobs. Strikes are still winning rights for workers around the world today.

WHERE IS EVERYBODY?

The People Desert Rome, 494-287 BCE

Much like Egypt, Rome was a very unequal society. A tiny group of rich and powerful men called the patricians made all the decisions and ensured that life was comfortable for themselves. Everybody else grew the vegetables, tended the animals, built the buildings, ran the shops and fought in the armies. These Romans, known as the plebeians, kept society going, but they had no say in how it was run. What they did have were their friendships, and the feeling that they should stand up for each other. The plebeians decided that they needed to join together to fight for their rights.

The plebeians realised that if all of them left the city at once, the patricians would notice how essential they were. So all the plebeians went to a nearby mountain until the patricians came to listen to what they had to say, and agreed to change things. It was decided that, for the first time, the plebeians would be represented by their own people in government.

They repeated their disappearing act – known as a secession – several more times, each time winning more rights, including a fairer legal system, the right to marry people from other classes, and the ability to be elected to the highest offices of government themselves.

THE FIGHT FOR FINERY
Women's March, Rome, 195 BCE

Life was tough for women in Ancient Rome. Whether they were rich or poor, they were told what to do. After a crushing defeat at the Battle of Cannae, the men passed a law called the Lex Oppia, banning women from wearing gold, jewellery and brightly-coloured clothes.

Clothes weren't just clothes — for rich women, dressing up was a way of showing you were as important as your husband and should be treated with respect (of course it wasn't the same for lower class women, who weren't treated with much respect anyway).

The women put up with 20 years of dowdiness. When the wars had ended and the economic crisis had passed, they expected to get their finery back, but this wasn't the men's priority. So the women flowed into the city, filling the streets and stopping any man who passed, demanding the ban be lifted. They were so annoying that eventually the men gave in and the women were free to dress the way they wanted again.

Noise

TACTICS

From singing to drumming, silence to rowdiness, people have used noise to unify, bring hope and make their voices heard.

MEDIEVAL BELLS, 1300s

In the English Peasants' Revolt, church bells were used for a new purpose. They could be heard far and wide, bringing the revolters together to plot on village greens.

SINGING REVOLUTION, 1991

The Baltic states had wanted to be free from Soviet rule for years. When huge crowds started singing national songs together, their movements gathered irresistible momentum, and soon Estonia, Latvia and Lithuania won their independence.

RUBBISH MUSIC, 2015

Going on a march in Syria can be dangerous, so instead protesters hid tiny speakers in rubbish bins and piles of manure all over Damascus. The police had to wade through the rubbish to turn off the illegal protest songs that were playing.

NEDA, 2009

When a protester called Neda was killed during the election protests in Iran, people wanted to share their feelings of sadness, but the government made it illegal to talk about her. Then the people remembered that because Neda is a common name, it appears in lots of Iranian pop songs. They started to use these as their ringtones, so whenever a phone rang, everyone would remember her.

PUSSY RIOT, 2012

A band of young women in neon stormed into an Orthodox cathedral in Moscow and started playing raucous feminist punk music. Pussy Riot ended up in prison, but this just made the band more famous and their messages about feminism, LGBTQ+ rights and other issues even louder.

FREEDOM SONGS, 1800s

On the plantations where they worked, enslaved Africans sang songs of resistance. Singing kept hope alive and spread secret messages about uprisings and routes of escape. The hymn 'Swing Low, Sweet Chariot' has a hidden meaning, the 'sweet chariot' referring to the Underground Railroad which rescued enslaved people: *a band of angels coming after me, coming for to carry me home*. (See also page 49.)

JAZZ NOT HATE, 2020

When a far-right politician started giving hate-filled speeches in Denmark, a group of jazz musicians decided to drown him out. Any time Rasmus Paludan was scheduled to speak, the musicians were there with their instruments, making more noise than him. They call themselves Denmark's "potentially biggest band" and specialise in bad music, so that anyone can join in whether or not they know how to play. Anyone, that is, except Paludan himself, who is the only person not invited to join the band.

SILENT PARADE, 1917

One of the first civil rights protests was a silent march. There was no chanting or singing: only the sombre sound of muffled drums could be heard as 10,000 African American men, women and children walked through the streets of New York. It was the absence of noise that amplified their grief in the wake of racist killings.

*The old world
is running up
like parchment
in the fire*

Medieval Troublemakers

WHOSE VILLAGE?

Kalabhra Revolt, India, 250-690 CE

In southern India, local kings wanted to thank their best warriors for winning so many wars for them. What better way to say thank you than with the gift of an entire village? Once they'd started giving villages away they couldn't stop, and soon teachers and priests were also receiving these over-the-top gifts.

Everyone was very pleased with this arrangement, except for the people who lived in these villages. The new owners made the residents pay them for the privilege of living where they had always lived. Before, the pastures, fisheries, forests and orchards belonged to everybody, but now everything had a price.

The landlords realised that these changes might not be popular, so they used their positions as teachers and priests to spread rumours among the villagers. They told them that anyone who disagreed with the new system would be punished by the gods.

The villagers weren't fooled for long, and soon they got together to take the landlords to court. Surely a judge would see how unfair things had become? But the landlords had friends in high places. The judges changed the laws, but not in the way the peasants had hoped. The new laws made it even harder for the villagers to use their land.

Now the villagers were more determined than ever. Every time the local king visited, they came out on the street pretending they were going to welcome him. When he got there, they greeted him with dramatic protests.

Thanks for coming! While you're here, give us our village back!

UNWELCOMING COMMITTEE

Eventually the villagers succeeded in taking back the land, but in turn they became just as brutal as those they had overthrown. Gaining power doesn't always guarantee a happy ending, and isn't the same as creating a world where everyone is equal.

This is an EMERGENCY!
Something VERY VERY important
has come up! Tools down everyone!
ALL HANDS ON DECK!
My embroidery threads are
becoming disorganised!

THE WAR OF THE SNAILS

Peasants' Revolt, Germany, 1524

The counts and countesses of 16th century Germany thought they were the most important people in the world. So when the Countess of Lupfen ran out of things to wind her embroidery thread on, she demanded that the peasant farmers who lived on her estates stop growing food and instead look for snail shells for her to use as spools for her yarn.

This was the last straw! It wasn't very fun to be a peasant – they didn't have much freedom and were given the most unpleasant jobs, like carrying dung around for their bosses. Even their rights to hunt, fish and chop wood on common land had been taken away. The peasants refused to work for the Countess anymore, and marched to a nearby town where they found others who felt the same way. Their sign was a shoe tied to a pole, symbolising their march towards freedom.

They spread secret messages and everyone helped out. The printing press, which had recently been invented a few towns away, helped them get the word out. They were creating the art of propaganda, and proving that peasants could read and think for themselves.

Count Lupfen started to get worried.

Count Lupfen thought he'd better do something to stop them getting even angrier. He made an agreement with the peasants to make some changes, but there were lots of strange rules that went with them. He didn't really want to change anything – he just wanted the peasants to calm down long enough for him to gather an army to crush the rebellion. The peasants didn't stand for it. Although many peasants were killed in the protests, they kept revolting.

Many of their castles were destroyed, but the counts and countesses managed to cling to power for a few more centuries. However, the peasants' struggles had not been in vain. Their spirit lived on in the revolts and revolutions that would radically change Europe over the next few centuries.

CONFOUND THE MIGHTY AND STRONG

The Levellers and the Diggers, England, 1640s

The 1640s were a turbulent time in England. Bad harvests and civil war led to great hardships, but because things had got so bad, old values were being questioned and it seemed like a new world was possible. People said "the old world was running up like parchment in the fire".*

The King believed that his power came directly from God, but people were starting to feel this was just an excuse for him to do whatever he wanted. By the 1640s he was being challenged from all sides.

The army generals and landlords wanted the country to be run by Parliament. In turn the landlords and army generals were having their authority challenged from below. The most radical ideas were coming from two groups called the Levellers and the Diggers.

The Levellers wanted everyone to be level. Power should come from the people, who deserved the right to vote, have their lands back, and practise whatever religion they chose. The Levellers had a manifesto and their own newspaper. They wore rosemary and sea-green ribbons in their hats so they could find each other when they met in the network of London pubs they called their 'offices'.

They were pretty organised and had thought a lot about the kind of society they wanted. But it was the Diggers who put their vision into action.

LEVELLERS

DIGGERS

*These words are originally attributed to Gerrard Winstanley, the leader of the Diggers.

33

One Sunday, while everyone was at Church, a group of Diggers walked onto a piece of common waste land and began to dig.

If they weren't going to be given power they would take it for themselves. They started planting corn and vegetables.

> Was the earth made to preserve a few men to live at ease, and for them to bag up the treasures of the earth, or was it made to preserve all her children?

GERRARD WINSTANLEY

The Diggers believed that the earth was a "common storehouse for all" and that by working together on the land they would grow the world they wanted to see.

The local lords of the manor saw the Diggers' camps
as a serious threat and raided them.

The Diggers survived these attacks for a whole year before being chased away.

Although they didn't manage to stay,
their ideas stuck.

The Levellers' Agreement of the People formed the basis of the
American Declaration of Independence more than a century later.

And living in the way they envisioned – as equals
in a fair community – was no small thing.

Even if it only lasted a year, they managed to create the world they had imagined.

Gardening

Martin Luther King Jr. said, "Even if I knew that tomorrow the world would go to pieces, I would still plant my apple tree". For many activists gardening and planting are acts of hope as well as ways to make change happen in the present.

GREEN GUERRILLAS, 1970s-90s

The Green Guerrillas turned unused corners of New York City into community gardens. But when the neighbourhoods became nicer to live in, the Mayor tried to make money by selling off the plots. The gardeners blocked traffic, carried plants into the road and gave children seeds to sow. For a few hours, streets became gardens. It was so much fun that the Green Guerrillas got the whole city on their side, and the gardens were saved.

WHEATFIELD, 1982

After the World Trade Center was built, a valuable plot of land next to it was left empty, which gave artist Agnes Denes an idea. Her next work of art wouldn't be a painting, but a real field of golden wheat. Growing it right there in New York's financial district would confront the inequality and hunger caused by capitalism. A group of people tended the field until the harvest was ready. Afterwards, the seeds travelled across the world to help grow the resistance.

POWER TO THE PEOPLE'S PARK, 1972

There was a barren patch of land on the University of California's Berkeley campus. Tired of waiting for permission to turn it into a park, the students did it themselves, sharing ideas about politics and the war in Vietnam as they gardened. When the government found out about this, they sent soldiers to shut down the park. First the students rioted. But the next time troops arrived, they tried flower power: 30,000 protesters greeted the soldiers and gave them each a daisy. The army left peacefully, no one was hurt, and the park is still there to this day.

GUERRILLA GARDENING, 2000s

Londoner Richard Reynolds started the Guerrilla Gardening movement in the UK by secretly sowing seeds in the disused planters outside his tower block. Next he covered the nearby roundabout with plants and soon people joined him. They took their trowels to places that needed help, like the village of Sipson, which was due to be bulldozed to make way for an airport runway. The gardeners helped residents put down roots in the village's empty spaces, to show that no one was going anywhere. Years of protesting have held the plans for the runway at bay.

BANANA OCCUPATION, 1995

When banana farmers in Tacamiche, Honduras, went on strike over low pay, the banana company decided to sell off the plantations. This meant that the workers would have nowhere to live and grow food, so they occupied the abandoned plantations and began to sow seeds. The banana bosses sent in bulldozers, but the occupiers stood their ground until the company and the government rebuilt the villages and gave them land for farming and fishing.

GREEN BELT, 1970s-

A woman named Wangari Maathai started the Green Belt Movement in response to deforestation in Kenya, helping hundreds of female farmers plant trees to stop the land becoming a desert. Planting trees inspired the women to take more action to protect the environment and fight government corruption. They have since grown over 30 million trees, saved land from development, and turned trees into a symbol of democracy.

Roll them up
like a carpet

Unsettling the Settlers

DISOBEDIENT DANCING
Native American Ghost Dance, Americas, 1890s

Since the first ships of Europeans arrived in the Americas in the 1400s, they had been trashing the place. They called it the 'New World', but it wasn't new. People had been living there for thousands of years. But the settlers clung to the fantasy that they had discovered an uninhabited paradise, and as they gradually moved west they destroyed the lives and lands of the Native Peoples. By the 1800s the settlers had created a whole way of life that aimed to wipe out the existing tribes and their relationship with the land.

The settlers did many cruel things in their ruthless pursuit of land. They purposefully spread diseases that killed whole communities, exterminated the buffalo and sent Native children to boarding schools where they would learn a language their parents didn't speak. Native chiefs were forced to sign treaties which took away their rights to live on their own land. Now they had to live on reservations where they weren't allowed to do the things which made them who they were.

The Native People have always fought back. Often forced to flee or use weapons in self defence, they also used many creative forms of nonviolent resistance. One of the most powerful of these was called the Ghost Dance. It began when a Paiute holy man named Wovoka had a vision of a land without settlers, where the Native way of life would flourish again. When they danced, people could share this vision too.

"The earth would roll up like a carpet with all the white man's ugly things – the stinking new animals, sheep and pigs, the fences, the telegraph poles, the mines and factories. Underneath would be the wonderful old-new world as it had been before the white fat-takers came…The white men will be rolled up, disappear, go back to their own continent…"*

*This is how Lakota leader Lame Deer described Wovoka's vision.

The reason for dancing went beyond disobedience. The visions they had when dancing inspired the dancers to live as if the settlers had never existed. The Ghost Dance became a movement, and camps were set up far away from the white settler towns. Ghost Dancers refused to take part in anything to do with settler culture, from speaking English to going to church and school. They stopped cutting their hair and wearing colonial-style clothes. But they did not stop dancing. It was total non-cooperation, and the settlers felt unsettled.

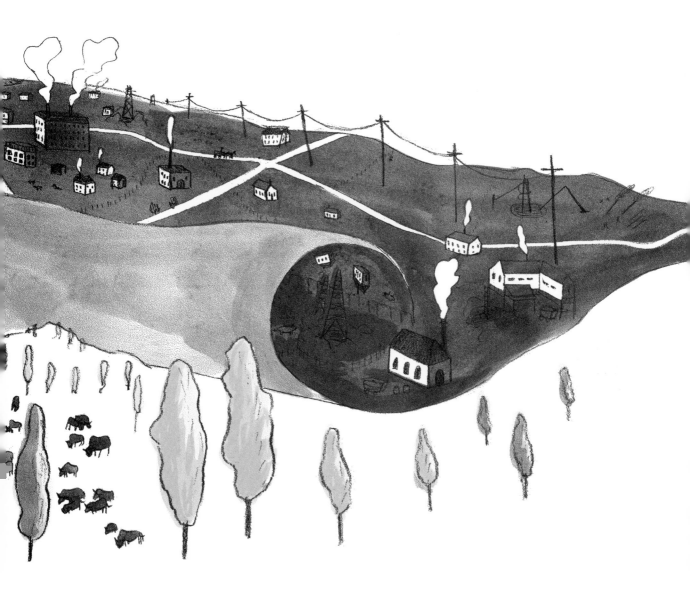

Refusing to play the settlers' game of violence and submission was more threatening than warfare. Eventually the settlers sent in the army, who surrounded the dancers at Wounded Knee creek. Over 300 Ghost Dancers were murdered in an act of inhumanity that will always be remembered by their descendants.

Most of what was taken from the Native Americans has never been given back. But the Ghost Dance was not danced in vain. While they danced, they created the world that they wanted to live in, even if it was repeatedly threatened. Instead of letting their way of life be smothered by the settlers, the dancers used the power of imagination to keep their culture alive.

PROTEST PLOUGHS
Māori Resistance, New Zealand, 1869-90s

Māori people had been living happily on the beautiful islands of New Zealand for hundreds of years before European explorers landed on their shores. The settlers brought new diseases and deadly weapons, and, just like the Europeans who had landed in America, a belief that the land was theirs to take. As the settler numbers grew, the Māori suffered more and more.

At first the Māori tried to fight for their land in battle, but they were outnumbered. Many of their people had been killed and it looked like the Europeans would take over the islands completely. It was at this lowest moment that a Māori man called Te Whiti was thinking about other ways his people could resist.

Te Whiti was one of the leaders of Parihaka, a community that he had founded to give the Māori people a safe place to live and tend the land. The Parihakans decided they wouldn't buy or use anything grown by the white farmers. Māori came from all over the country to live there, bringing their ploughs with them so they could grow their own food. Te Whiti said they could stay as long as they gave up their weapons.

One day, Te Whiti made a big announcement to the settlers.

The Europeans didn't believe the Māori could harm them without using weapons. They went home feeling very relaxed and pleased with themselves. They continued to expand their farmland into Māori territory, sending surveyors out to measure up the land and find the best bits. They drove right through the middle of the Māori's crops and marked off the places they were planning to steal.

Soon Parihaka was almost the only place left that had not been taken by the settlers. As the surveyors got closer, the Parihakan people gathered together to come up with a plan. In the old days they might have tried to fight the surveyors off, but in the new spirit of peaceful resistance, they did something much sneakier. While they were looking the other way, the Parihakans quietly removed the surveyors' measuring instruments, folded up the tents and drove everything away.

Then one morning, the neighbouring white farmers got up to start the day as usual, but this was no ordinary morning.

As far as the eye could see, Parihakan farmers had brought out their ploughs to work the land that had been stolen from them.

The Māori just smiled, ignoring the farmers as they continued to plough.

The settlers started arresting the ploughers, but for every plougher who was taken off the land, another stepped in to take their place.

The government couldn't believe what was happening. They sent in the army and ended up spending almost a million pounds trying to remove the peaceful ploughers of Parihaka.

Despite everything the Parihakans remained committed to nonviolent resistance, baffling the soldiers, who didn't know how to fight people who refused to fight back.

Sorry for the inconvenience!

Although the Māori were never given all their land back, they did survive as a people, and their creative resistance is recognised as the reason why.

FOLLOW THE NORTH STAR
Fighting Slavery, Africa, Americas and Europe, 1400s-1800s

European colonisers didn't just take land. They also saw people as property they could buy, sell and steal. When European traders set up sugar plantations in West Africa, instead of paying the local people to tend their fields, they forced them to work for free.

Soon they were marching Africans onto ships bound for the Americas. Millions of enslaved people were sailed thousands of miles in horrifically cramped, dangerous conditions. Many died on the journey. Those who didn't arrived to a terrible fate, usually separated from their friends and family and put to work on plantations growing sugar, coffee, tobacco, cotton and cocoa.

From the very beginning, there was resistance. Some enslaved Africans were able to escape while the ships were still in the harbour. Warriors came out of the forests in rafts to rescue their kidnapped friends, and enslaved people set fire to ships while their kidnappers were trading on the shore.

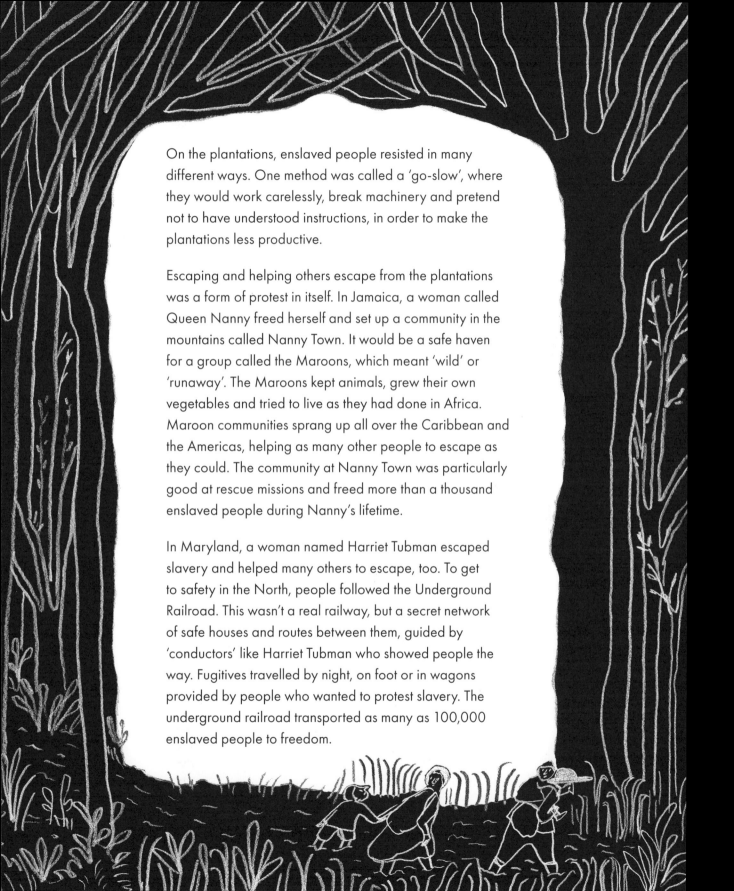

On the plantations, enslaved people resisted in many different ways. One method was called a 'go-slow', where they would work carelessly, break machinery and pretend not to have understood instructions, in order to make the plantations less productive.

Escaping and helping others escape from the plantations was a form of protest in itself. In Jamaica, a woman called Queen Nanny freed herself and set up a community in the mountains called Nanny Town. It would be a safe haven for a group called the Maroons, which meant 'wild' or 'runaway'. The Maroons kept animals, grew their own vegetables and tried to live as they had done in Africa. Maroon communities sprang up all over the Caribbean and the Americas, helping as many other people to escape as they could. The community at Nanny Town was particularly good at rescue missions and freed more than a thousand enslaved people during Nanny's lifetime.

In Maryland, a woman named Harriet Tubman escaped slavery and helped many others to escape, too. To get to safety in the North, people followed the Underground Railroad. This wasn't a real railway, but a secret network of safe houses and routes between them, guided by 'conductors' like Harriet Tubman who showed people the way. Fugitives travelled by night, on foot or in wagons provided by people who wanted to protest slavery. The underground railroad transported as many as 100,000 enslaved people to freedom.

In their cosy homes in Britain, many people drinking hot chocolate and smoking pipes in their cotton pyjamas didn't want to know about the terrible human cost of their comforts. But others were working hard to wake them to the horrors of slavery. When writers like Olaudah Equiano, Quobna Ottobah Cugoano and Mary Prince toured Britain talking about their experiences of slavery, people started to think about where the things they used came from and who had made them.

Outrage spread fast as audiences spoke to their friends about what they had heard. Supporters of the cause wore anti-slavery brooches and decided to stop using the sugar that was produced by enslaved people.

Soon the movement to abolish slavery was supported by many different kinds of people. Factory workers in Lancashire refused to spin cotton produced by enslaved people. In London, clergymen and Members of Parliament (MPs) made speeches, lawyers took on cases, and Mary Prince became the first woman to present an anti-slavery petition to Parliament. Slavery had become an issue no one could ignore. In 1807, after centuries of doing the wrong thing, the British government finally agreed it would end its involvement in the transatlantic slave trade, and in 1833 passed an Act to abolish slavery throughout the British Empire.

MARY PRINCE

It was night when I reached my new home... The stones and the timber were the best things in it; they were not so hard as the hearts of the owners

In America, many different campaigners were also working together to end slavery. Abolitionists like Frederick Douglass, Sojourner Truth and Henry Box Brown, who had freed themselves from slavery* delivered powerful protest speeches and inspired people to join them.

Eventually in 1865 the United States Constitution was amended to abolish slavery. The abolitionists had won, but they knew they still had far to go. Without basic human rights, African Americans couldn't be considered free.

Many abolitionists went on to campaign for the right to vote. The fight for equal rights and against racism has continued through the civil rights movement and into recent Black Lives Matter protests.

*Henry Box Brown escaped by posting himself in a wooden box to abolitionists in Philadelphia.

Words

Writing can be its own form of activism. So can reading!

INSPIRING INK, 1792

Although she never used the word, author Mary Wollstonecraft wrote one of the first ever books on feminism. *The Vindication of the Rights of Women* was a powerful argument that women should receive the same education, rights and respect as men. Although Wollstonecraft died shortly after publishing the book, it lived on. Her book was inspired by writings that came out of the recent French Revolution and in turn inspired the founders of the women's suffrage movement. She continues to inspire feminists today.

REBELLIOUS READING, 2014

When a military dictatorship took over, surveillance and censorship made people in Thailand feel like they were living in George Orwell's dystopian novel *1984*. The new army-run government called itself the National Council for Peace and Order, just like in the book, where the 'Ministry of Peace' is actually responsible for war. Gatherings of more than five people were banned, so instead protesters adopted a symbol of their discontent: a copy of *1984*. Silently reading the book on trains and benches signalled that they were watching the government as much as it was watching them.

ABOLITIONIST AUTHORS, 1700s-1800s

When formerly enslaved Africans like Mary Prince, Olaudah Equiano and Frederick Douglass wrote accounts of their experiences both in and beyond slavery, the reality of what was happening on plantations came to life for their readers. These first-hand accounts of what it was like to be enslaved caused several British and American people to finally change their position on slavery and join the abolitionist movement.

REVENGE OF THE BORROWERS, 2011

Borrowers at Stony Stratford library in the UK found out their library was being closed. The government cut its funding, thinking no one needed books any more. One Saturday, instead of taking one or two books home as usual, each borrower took their full allowance – 15 books each. The aim was to clear the shelves completely, to show just how many people loved and used the library. The last book to go, just before closing time, was *The Borrowers* by Mary Norton. The protest worked and the library was saved.

THE LESBIAN AVENGER HANDBOOK, 1992

The Lesbian Avengers were set up to talk loudly and proudly about lesbian issues. Together they wrote a handbook about setting up your own group, running meetings and organising protests. The 'Handy Guide to Homemade Revolution' helped over 50 chapters of Lesbian Avengers take the US by storm.

SILENT SPRING, 1962

Scientist Rachel Carson noticed that a chemical called DDT was causing birds to die, no longer filling the countryside with song. She took action by publishing *Silent Spring*, her beautifully written but shocking book about the terrible effect pesticides were having on the environment. The response to the book was so strong that DDT was banned in the USA, and a whole new environmental movement sprang up around it.

SPEAKING YOUR TRUTH, 1960s-70s

Writers like James Baldwin, Audre Lorde and Maya Angelou were part of the Black Arts Movement, using literature to reflect on race, class, gender and sexuality in America. Activists in their writing, they were also activists on the ground. They organised protests, raised funds, and whenever they were asked to read their work aloud they spoke about politics. Creating a new language, authors opened dialogues and pushed conversations forward. As Lorde wrote, "only one thing is more frightening than speaking your truth. And that is not speaking."

Ye are many,
they are few

CATCH THE KING!

The French Revolution, France, 1789-99

In 1789 French people had a lot to complain about.

The country had been at war for what seemed like hundreds of years. All the money had been going to buy warships for the King and new dresses for the Queen. Meanwhile ordinary people had to save up a week's wages just to buy a loaf of bread.

People were hungry and angry. They exploded onto the streets of Paris, fired up to change things. They were staying up all night scheming in cafés, handing out pamphlets and even publishing their own newspapers full of ideas about how to create a new France that would put the people first.

King Louis XVI and Queen Marie-Antoinette thought that if they hid in their Palace at Versailles, just outside Paris, it would all blow over. They had plenty to entertain themselves: tennis courts, a theatre and a hall of mirrors that reflected their three-foot-tall hairstyles back at them thousands of times over. The Queen even had a model village in the grounds where she and her friends liked to pretend to be poor country peasants.

The people weren't having it and set off to Versailles. Women led the march, knowing the King's guards wouldn't start a fight with a bunch of ladies in skirts. They were right. No one stopped them, and when they arrived at the Palace they took the surprised King and Queen hostage and marched them back to Paris with their wigs askew.

Bringing the royal family to the heart of the city, where they would be among ordinary people, showed the protesters that they could do anything. Every day the streets filled with revolutionaries finding new ways to make their voices heard and turning up in huge numbers to confront the powerful at churches, government buildings and prisons. Knowing that big crowds showed strength, protesters often interrupted theatre performances, calling on the audience to come and be part of the drama unfolding on the streets.

Amid all the protests, the King kept trying to escape. But the people were very good at catching him. When he was next driven back to Paris, the crowds turned their backs as the carriage passed. A group of boys climbed a statue of Louis' father and blindfolded it. This daring action, which would have been an unthinkable insult even a year before, was the people's way of telling Louis that even his dad would be ashamed of how he was behaving.

Louis knew that the people were in charge now, and three months later he officially handed his power over to them. But the people wanted to go further. They didn't believe in royalty anymore – and it wasn't long before Louis and Marie-Antoinette's heads were chopped off.

Although it's often remembered as a violent time, most of the events of the French Revolution were peaceful. It was the start of a movement of people taking power back from kings and queens in many different countries and inventing new ways to rule themselves. The forms of protest that were invented during the Revolution have been used ever since to make change happen all over the world.

COME ARMED WITH YOUR CONSCIENCE
Peterloo, UK, 1819

All over Europe, people were sick and tired of the inequality that meant the rich hunted and banqueted while poor families could barely put dinner on the table. People often had to sell off their furniture and clothes just to be able to buy bread. Factories were springing up all over the North of England, where people were losing their jobs to new machines that could work faster than humans.

If only everyone could vote. Then they could have a say in how things were run. But the only people who did have a vote were a tiny group of rich men who already had plenty.

People knew things weren't right and tried to show it. Though they signed petitions, went on strike and even smashed machinery, it felt like nothing was changing. But people were meeting each other and exchanging ideas – and every meeting was bigger than the last.

Plans were made for a big summer gathering in Manchester to listen to inspiring speakers and talk about how they could get their own Member of Parliament to represent them in government. They didn't want to bring down the government – they just wanted to make it work for them too.

It was a sunny day in August, and people dressed in their Sunday best to walk to St Peter's Field in the middle of town. Bands were playing and people were carrying banners and picnics. None of the meetings had ever come close to the size of this – over half the city was there!

It couldn't have been a more peaceful gathering. But instead of seeing the friendly crowd in front of their eyes, the government imagined they had another French Revolution on their hands. They hastily gathered together a group of men from the local pubs and sent them into the crowd on horseback.

The peaceful gathering soon turned to tragedy as the crowd was attacked by the drunken, untrained army. Those who had fought in the recent Napoleonic Wars said that what happened that day was worse than the Battle of Waterloo, and it was nicknamed Peterloo.

Outrage spread fast, bringing the cause to the nation's attention, and people say this is where true democracy began in Britain. A wave of social change was underway. Soon Manchester had its own Member of Parliament, and over the next century more and more people were granted the vote.

MAY I HAVE A DAY OFF?

May Day, Global, Pre-history to the present

Thousands of years ago, as spring arrived and green shoots appeared above the ground, the people of Northern Europe would emerge from their homes and greet each other after the long winter. By May, it was warm enough to gather together outside for the first time since the autumn. They marked the return of the sun with a celebration called Beltane, which means Day of Fire.

From that time onwards, the 1st of May became May Day – a special day of feasting and dancing around the Maypole. A day when the normal order of things was turned on its head, when people took time off from their usual roles in society, dressed up and made fun of rulers and lords.

Eventually this day of freedom became a day when workers protested. During the French Revolution, it was a way for radical ideas to spread throughout the countryside. Maypoles got bigger and festivals more rowdy. The ribbons that had always decorated the Maypole were now painted with slogans like 'NO MORE RENTS!', and people stole things from the houses of the rich to burn on the bonfire.

In the 1880s a famous strike was held on May Day in Chicago. There, it was common for people to work 16-hour shifts, six days a week, leaving barely any time for rest or fun – while others were unemployed and couldn't afford to feed their families. If those with jobs worked a bit less, there would be more employment and wages to go round. So thousands of workers put down their tools, demanding an eight-hour working day.

One of the strike leaders was a woman of colour called Lucy Parsons. She asked people to sit down in their factories and stop work. That day, Chicago was brought to a standstill.

In honour of this historic strike, a group of international workers decided to come together on the 1st of May 1890 to demand an eight-hour day for everyone.

In villages and towns, people came out onto the streets with garlands of flowers, banners, musical instruments and their families. Hundreds of thousands of people stopped work to protest and celebrate being together.

In the US, President Eisenhower was so concerned about the collective power of the strikers that in 1958 he suggested an alternative to May Day – 'Law and Order Day' – when the workers would be good and obey orders all day long. But May Day just got bigger. People kept protesting, and the eight-hour day was won in many countries, from Chile and Austria to Japan and New Zealand.

May Day remains an important date for protesting about working conditions, hours and pay, as well as for learning about and celebrating radical ideas.

8 HOURS WORK
8 HOURS REST
8 HOURS FOR WHAT YOU WILL

Doing nothing

From strikes to sit-ins, non-cooperation is one of the most effective forms of civil disobedience. As well as interrupting business as usual, actively doing nothing can create powerful imagery of stillness and peace.

BED PEACE, HAIR PEACE, 1969

When 1960s superstars John Lennon and Yoko Ono decided to get married, the idea of millions of paparazzi at their wedding was almost enough to put them off. Instead they decided to do something useful with the publicity, turning their honeymoon into a protest against the Vietnam War. Every day for a week, they invited photographers and journalists into their hotel room, where they lay in bed beneath posters which said "Hair Peace" and "Bed Peace". Anyone who printed the photos would also be printing a statement against the war. By doing nothing, John and Yoko weren't just calling for peace, they were demonstrating it.

SIT-OFF, 1930

During the fight for Indian independence, protesters made their own salt to avoid paying tax to the British. When word got out that an Indian salt depot was about to be raided by the British colonial government, a group sat down in front of the doors. As they made themselves comfortable for a long night of peaceful salt-guarding, the police sat down too. "We're going to stay here as long as you do," they told the protesters. The police lasted 28 hours – not long enough to out-sit the seasoned protesters. The salt was saved.

'POLITE PROCRASTINATION', 1940s

Hitler wanted Nazi Germany to develop an atomic bomb, which could have destroyed huge swathes of the planet. German scientists were ordered to research nuclear weapons, but although they enthusiastically nodded along, they had already decided to do their jobs very badly. They kept vital plans and information hidden away, and whenever they were called on to report on progress, they told their bosses how difficult the task was. By secretly refusing to do their jobs, they made sure no one could develop deadly nuclear weapons while Hitler was in power.

STANDING MAN, 2013

Protests had been going on for weeks in Taksim Square, Istanbul. A demonstration against the removal of trees in nearby Gezi Park and plans to demolish the square's much-loved Cultural Centre had turned into unrest over how the whole country was being governed. Protesters were eventually removed, and when artist Erdem Gündüz arrived, the square was empty. Gündüz just stood in silence, looking towards the Cultural Centre. Hours passed and he didn't move. Gradually, people came to join him. The image of hundreds of people standing deadly still, staring at the building they wanted to save and all that it represented, won even more citizens to the cause.

SICK-IN, 1600s-1800s & 1950s

Enslaved Africans forced to work on plantations in the Americas pioneered the use of the sick-in. Without any legal protections, pretending to be ill was a way to get time off from relentless work, and also reduced their enslavers' profits – if an enslaved person was being sold, they might fake a disability or illness to deliberately lower their price. The tactic was also used in China in the 1950s, where workers were unhappy with their conditions but had no union to fight for their rights. Instead, workers took as many sick days as possible, reporting unusual symptoms, staying in bed, and resulting in a drop in production.

SLEEPING VETERANS, 1971

When American soldiers came back from the Vietnam War, many were traumatised by the terrible things they had seen and been ordered to do. They planned a week-long protest on the National Mall near the White House, where they would talk about their experience, demonstrate, and even turn themselves in to the police as war criminals. The government allowed them to stay, as long as they didn't sleep there, even though many returning soldiers had nowhere else to sleep. The activists broke the law and slept there anyway, turning rest into a political action, highlighting the bad dreams and sleepless nights the war had caused them.

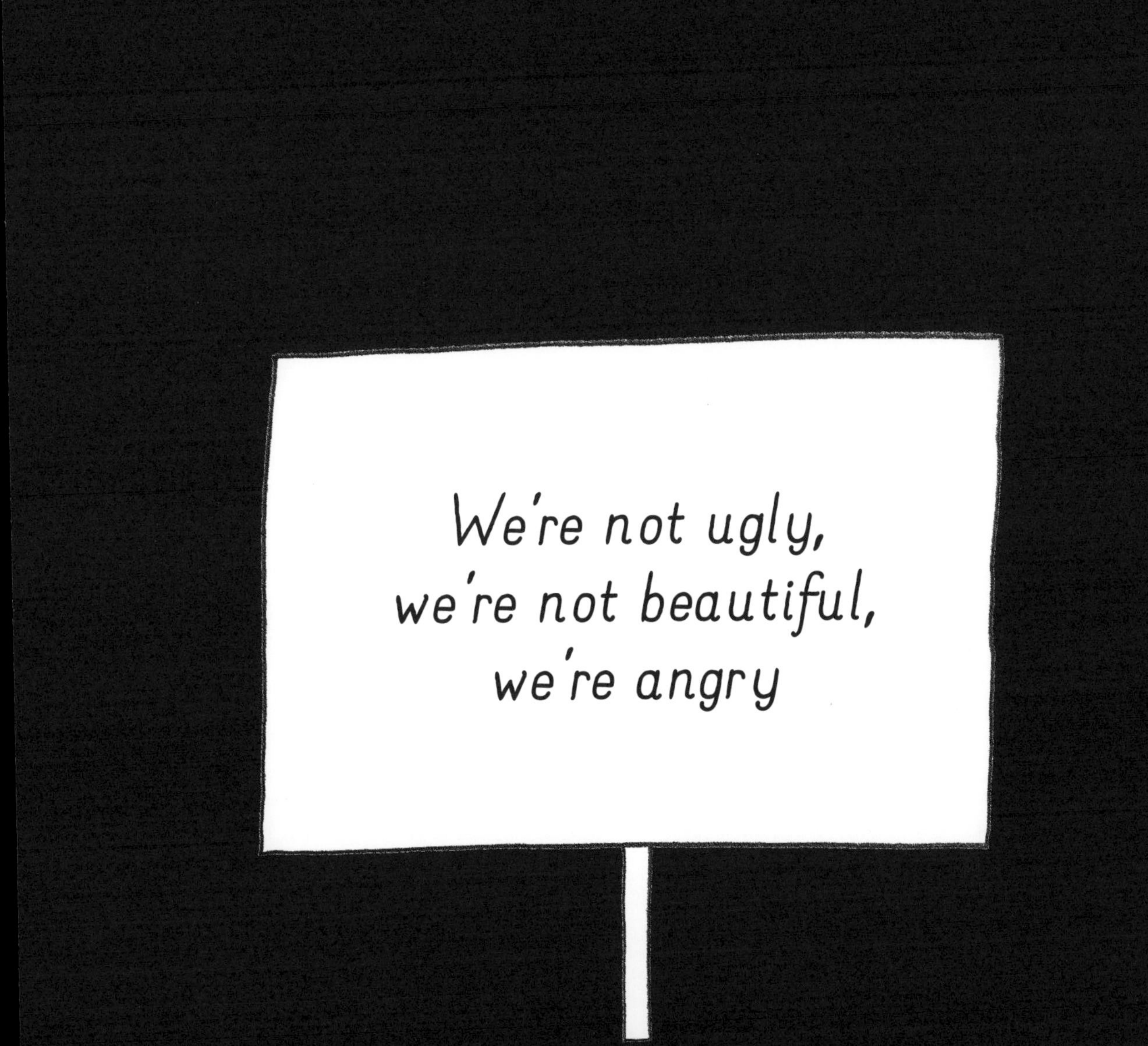
We're not ugly,
we're not beautiful,
we're angry

Welcome to this men's meeting for discussing men's issues – also known as "politics"

DEEDS NOT WORDS
The Suffragettes, UK, 1900s

Women had been fighting for the vote (known as suffrage) in the UK for a very long time. They petitioned and campaigned nicely and got close to changing the law a few times, yet their male representatives in Parliament always found a way to wriggle out of giving them the vote at the last minute. Some women thought this meant they should keep prodding politely, but for others it was time for a complete change in tactics.

A group of women* decided that if they weren't being listened to, they would speak louder. In the run up to an election in 1905, two members of the group smuggled a banner into a political meeting. They stood up and interrupted, repeatedly asking when they would be given the vote. Their bravery got them arrested – it was simply too outrageous that women would speak out in public. Far from stopping them, spending the night in prison made their cause famous and inspired more women to join them in taking action.

Their group grew bigger and bigger and soon they were able to hold huge marches that showed just how many women were part of this new disobedient force. When a newspaper mocked them with the girly nickname 'Suffragettes', they adopted this new identity which marked them out as different from the well-behaved group called the Suffragists. Their sense of humour was as fierce as their bravery.

*They called themselves the Women's Social and Political Union (WSPU for short)

As their numbers swelled, so did the variety of actions they took. Before long, they were disrupting everything with their rebellious spirit. Being a Suffragette was not just a political stance. It was a community and a way for women to live bigger, bolder lives in a world where everything was designed to silence their creativity and intelligence. Ignoring them was no longer an option.

They weren't afraid of breaking the law, in fact that was one of their tactics. They even learned Suffrajitsu – special self-defence moves they could use if they were attacked by the police. Being in prison was a traumatic experience, especially as many of them went on hunger strike and were force-fed. They were welcomed on their release by other Suffragettes, who gave them medals to recognise their bravery. Being prepared to go to prison meant they could be more daring in their actions.

Here are just a few of the things they did that eventually won them the vote:

Chained themselves to the railings outside Parliament...

... giving them time to make speeches while the police cut through their chains.

Sent themselves as 'human letters' to the Prime Minister, delivered by post to Downing Street.

Stormed Parliament...

... thousands of them banging at the door so loudly that they could be heard by the politicians inside.

Hid in a furniture van on its way into Parliament. Two Suffragettes managed to get into the chamber where they shouted their slogans at the MPs.

Held theatrical pageants...

... dressing up as famous women as a reminder of how powerful women had been throughout history.

Disrupted the postal system – the main way that people communicated...

... pouring jam, ink and acid into postboxes and sometimes even setting them on fire.

Made sure politicans kept the message in mind even when they were relaxing...

... by burning their slogans into golf courses.

Chalked slogans on pavements.

Smashed windows in buildings all over London using tiny hammers that were meant for breaking toffee...

DEPARTMENT STORE

... in protest at the Prime Minister yet again sabotaging a bill that would have given them the right to vote.

THE WOMEN TAKE DOWN THE KING

The Abeokuta Women's Revolt, Nigeria, 1940s

In southern Nigeria women had been used to a more equal way of life. Growing food and selling it at the markets gave them independence from men. Their strong community networks helped them pass on messages and stand up for each other in times of trouble. And they also played a part in politics, having a say in the way society was run.

This all changed with the arrival of the British who were taking land in Africa, just as they had in America, New Zealand, India, and many other places around the world. The British quickly tried to make West African life more like the society they were used to at home, putting men in charge and ignoring the women.

No sooner had the British taken away the women's power than they brought in taxes that made women pay more than anybody else. Suddenly there were all sorts of weird new fines for things like not sweeping the front of your house. King Ladapo Ademola was in charge of collecting these taxes for the British, relishing his new power and the money that came with it.

A headteacher named Funmilayo Ransome-Kuti in the town of Abeokuta was angry about what was happening to her fellow women. So she set up the Abeokuta Ladies' Club to stop the government taxing the market women.

As they became more political they changed the name to Abeokuta Women's Union and announced that any woman from any walk of life could join. Immediately, hundreds of thousands of women signed up. Now they set their sights higher. As well as ending the unfair taxes they vowed to challenge colonial rule, and make sure they were represented in government.

The women gradually escalated their activities. When a petition to the King didn't work, they hired an accountant who revealed how corrupt he was. Many women stopped paying their taxes in protest, and Funmilayo travelled to England to speak to the press and the British government.

Because the King was still ignoring them, the women started protesting outside his palace. A thousand of them showed up on the first day. The next time 10,000 women came, and sang songs that made fun of the King. Many of them were arrested, but the women weren't afraid. They had a plan. Next time they would camp outside the palace – and wouldn't leave until their friends were released. Now there were 50,000 of them! Eventually the King's chiefs realised who the winning team was. They sided with the protesters, stopping the taxes and putting the first women into government. The King had no choice but to give up his throne. The women had won.

Funmilayo Ransome-Kuti spent the rest of her life fighting for Nigerian women and went on to become the first female chief in Nigeria's Western House of Chiefs.

WOMEN UNITE
Women's Liberation Movement, Global, 1970s-

In 1970, the women's liberation movement was just beginning in Britain. The vote had been won 40 years previously, but the fight wasn't over: it was time for a second wave of feminism. Women wanted to be respected and safe from sexism and violence, they wanted equal choices, equal pay and equal power, and they wanted to be judged on things other than their looks.

When that year's Miss World contest rolled around as it did every year, a group of activists decided it was time to do something. They bought tickets to the prize-giving ceremony, dressed up in their most glamorous clothes and sat down to watch the contestants parading around in swimming costumes and evening wear. No one suspected the activists were anything other than ordinary audience members enjoying a normal sexist evening out. But when all the contestants had safely left the stage, leaving just the host telling offensive jokes, the feminists sprang into action. They flung flour-bombs off the balcony, scattered leaflets in the stalls and used water-pistols to soak the security guards in ink.

As they were carried away by the police, the protesters knew that they had made their mark: 100 million television viewers were watching the contest worldwide, and many more were talking about it the next day. The words Women's Liberation entered households of people who didn't know there was a dynamic new movement standing up for the rights of women.

And all around the world, feminists were taking action in their own ways.

In Japan, a group called Chūpiren, also known as the Pink Panthers, were noted for their striking protests. Wearing pink hardhats and white suits they marched for sexual and gender equality, even storming into the offices of cheating husbands.

During the Vietnam War, the Committee of Women was formed by Vietnamese women to help protect them against violence. The women organised protests secretly: groups would arrive in town as if they were going shopping, then all of a sudden they would whip off their scarves and tie them to their walking sticks, turning them into banners emblazoned with slogans against the American occupation. If some protesters were arrested, others would sit outside the jails with their noisy children and babies for hours, making such a racket that the prison guards had to give in and release their friends.

In the USA, protesters made a huge 'Freedom Trash Can', and spent the day throwing in symbols of female oppression like pots and pans, bras and false eyelashes.

More recently in Zimbabwe, feminists fought back against being harassed on the street by organising a Miniskirt March in 2014. Zimbabwean women, like other women around the world, were sick of being told that the way they dressed was responsible for sexist catcalls and violence against women. By taking over the streets and dressing as they pleased, they sparked a national conversation about sexual harassment.

Transport

The ways we get around – by bike, car, train or bus – can be an ideal way to focus attention on an issue. Activists have used transport to bring people together, disrupt daily life, and reimagine cities.

NO BARRIERS, 2012

Subway fares were rising in New York City, workers were being paid less, and dodging the unaffordable fares often landed young people of colour in jail. Across the subway, workers and activists chained subway gates open, put up official-looking signs saying "Free Entry, No Fares Collected. Please Enter Through the Service Gate" and encouraged passengers to walk straight through. This generous action got people thinking about how things could be different.

SLOW CHANGE, 1983

Anyone protesting in Chile under the dictator Pinochet risked arrest and torture, so a lot of people stayed quiet. But then they discovered that staying quiet and doing less could also help make their feelings known. On the first National Day of Protest taxis began to drive at half their normal speed, and soon everyone was moving slowly – in cars, buses or on foot. No one could be arrested just for going slowly, and when they saw others shuffling along, they knew they weren't alone. This sneakily open way of protesting helped people believe that change would come eventually, however slowly – and it did.

FREE RIDES, 2018

When bus drivers' jobs were threatened in the city of Okayama, Japan, they wanted to strike, but knew this would make things difficult for the ordinary people who relied on the bus service. Instead they continued to drive the buses, but let passengers ride for free – so people would get to work, but the bus companies wouldn't get the fares. This brought the drivers huge public support and media attention.

ROAD BLOCK, 1971

Protesters decided that the only way to stop the Vietnam War was to stop the government. They designed and printed a map of Washington D.C. showing all the places roads could be blocked so government officials couldn't get to work. On the day of action, 25,000 young people arrived, but before they could block the traffic nearly a third of them were handcuffed in the biggest mass arrest in US history. Though the city wasn't shut down, the plans alone got the government wondering whether ending the war would be better than provoking chaos and disorder at home.

BUS LOCK-ON, 2010s

Disabled People Against Cuts is a UK-based group of Disabled activists fighting government cuts to the benefits and services they depend on. They have blocked roads by locking wheelchairs together, while others have locked wheelchairs onto buses. Disrupting traffic in this way highlights the disruption that government cuts have caused to Disabled people's lives.

CYCLING SUFFRAGETTES, 1900s

Cycling was considered unsuitable for women, and many men were worried that if women got a taste of freedom on two wheels they might never come back to make them their dinner. So for the Suffragettes, getting on a bike was a form of protest in itself – and also meant being able to get to meetings without having to ask a man to take them there. Cyclists could deliver leaflets further afield, and make quick getaways from their illegal actions. A special bicycle was even designed in the Suffragette colours of purple, white and green.

CLOWN COPS, 1990s

When Antanas Mockus became Mayor of Bogotá he was determined to turn the dangerous, corrupt city into a friendly community. He started with the traffic police, who let aggressive drivers cause chaos. Instead of hiring more police, Mockus fired them – offering them their jobs back if they retrained as mime artists. Soon the streets were filled with painted faces and silly costumes. The mimes made fun of bad driving, praised good driving, and helped people cross the street. Co-operating and laughing together opened people's imaginations about how their city could change for the better.

Truth Force

Independence and Resistance

TO THE SEA!
Salt March, India, 1930

Since the 1600s, British rulers had been competing with other European countries for control of India, which to them was just a giant storehouse full of lovely things that they could take and sell back at home, like spices, tea and silk. The British grip tightened until they officially ruled over the whole of India. They called it the jewel in their crown.

The Indians didn't want to be anybody's jewel. They started a long campaign for independence, organising boycotts, protests and strikes. But then a man named Mohandas Gandhi shared a new way of taking action. He knew the Indians needed to fight harder, but they would never win against the British in a war. The Indians would have to fight without violence.

To describe his nonviolent tactics, Gandhi came up with the Sanskrit word 'satyagraha', which means 'Truth Force' in English. It was more than refusing to fight – it meant showing active strength in the face of oppression.

Gandhi had spent many years studying the way campaigns could be won. He realised that to capture the imagination of the whole country, he had to focus the campaign on something small and practical. One of the ways the British were making life harder in India was by making people pay huge taxes every time they bought salt. So Gandhi announced that he was going to walk to the sea to make his own.

Gandhi and the 77 people he'd persuaded to join him didn't seem like much of a threat to the British empire. But they walked through villages on their way, giving speeches about Indian independence and inspiring people to join the march. By the time they reached the sea, there were 12,000 of them.

India now had a nonviolent army of peaceful protesters ready to take on the entire British occupation. They set up their own salt works, boycotted British cloth and alcohol, and quit their government jobs.

In just a few months, the British were so shaken that they invited Gandhi to a meeting and began to negotiate. The meeting itself was the first victory: until then the British had never taken the Indian point of view seriously. The door to self-rule had been pushed ajar and now it was just a matter of how and when the British would leave. In 1947, India celebrated its independence.

Gandhi wasn't a perfect person and didn't always support equality for everyone. Nevertheless, his ideas about nonviolence have given birth to some of the most successful movements of the 20th century, and continue to inspire protesters today.

GUTEN TAG!

Resisting the Nazis, Europe, 1930s-40s

In the 1930s Adolf Hitler rose to power in Germany as the head of the Nazi party. This was terrifying news, especially for Jewish people, and also for Roma people, LGBTQ+ people, Disabled people, and anyone who didn't conform to Hitler's twisted idea of what a human should be. Nazi soldiers rounded up anyone belonging to these groups and sent them to concentration camps. Six million Jews and many other people were murdered in what is known as the Holocaust.

As the Nazis invaded neighbouring countries in Europe, threatening their communities too, other countries united to fight back, declaring war against Germany in 1939. The story of World War II is well known. Less often spoken about are the many nonviolent ways that people successfully resisted the Nazis.

Jewish people were made to wear yellow stars, which marked them out as different and made them targets for Nazi violence. To show their solidarity and make the system less effective, some non-Jewish people started wearing yellow stars too. In Hungary, schoolgirls sewed yellow stars to their uniforms to protect their Jewish classmates. There were lots of ways people gave secret signals to each other without obviously breaking the law, which would have had terrible consequences.

Posters were secretly put up in Rotterdam reminding people to be kind to their Jewish friends. Anti-Nazi graffiti by a group of young boys called The Little Wolves appeared all over Warsaw.

One day all the Jewish people in Berlin who hadn't already been taken away were rounded up. But many of them were married to non-Jewish people, who were left behind.

Six thousand wives followed the trucks to the building where their husbands were being held. They surrounded the gates, calling to their husbands and shouting for them to be set free.

The men were so pleased to hear their wives' voices that, though it was forbidden, they came to the windows to see them and show that they were there.

The police did not know what to do. Whenever they managed to disperse the crowd, the women would return moments later. The only way to get rid of the wives was to give in, and within a few hours they released all the men.

Meanwhile, Norwegians wore paperclips to symbolise keeping together, and on trains and trams, passengers refused to sit next to German soldiers. This upset the soldiers so much that it was made illegal not to sit down if there was a seat available! Doctors in Germany provided notes excusing young men from joining the army. Their sympathy to the resistance could be recognised by the way they greeted their patients, saying "Guten Tag" instead of "Heil Hitler".

Teachers in Scandinavia went a step further and refused outright to teach Nazi lessons of hatred. Because of their disobedience, the Nazis closed all schools for a month. So teachers invited children to their homes and taught them in secret.

A thousand teachers were taken to prison for refusing to do as they were told, but their fellow educators were not frightened into giving in. The schools were eventually reopened, the prisoners were released and the teachers were allowed to teach what they wanted.

POTS AND PANS
Cacerolazo, Chile, 1971-73

The housewives of Chile looked in their cupboards. They had cooked all the vegetables, all the rice and all the beans. All they had left were empty pots and pans. Protesting was not something many of these women had done or even thought about before. But food shortages and rationing had been getting worse and the women knew if they didn't do something their families would go hungry.

So they picked up their saucepans and walked outside. As the women started banging their pots with wooden spoons, more people came out onto the streets to see what was happening. Soon their children were joining in, and the neighbourhoods were filled with the sounds of drumming. Busy mothers and elderly grandmothers who couldn't leave their homes joined from their kitchen windows.

The unmistakable sound of protest was heard everywhere. The noise spread fast and was hard for the police to control. Pots and pans became the voice of the people until the government could no longer ignore their demands. Soon cacerolazos – which means 'hitting stew pots' – were happening across South America as the quickest and easiest way to make a political statement.

This was not the first time people had banged pots to make a point. In medieval folk traditions, peasants would parade through the village hitting pans to show their disapproval of anything from inappropriate marriages to local bullies.

In recent decades cacerolazos have been used successfully in other parts of the world. Icelandic protesters thumped pans to interrupt meetings at Parliament and were successful in gaining a new government in their 'Kitchenware Revolution'. In Quebec, students hit pots every night until tuition fees were lowered. And during the Covid-19 pandemic people all over the world drummed with spoons from their windows and doorsteps. Making noise together in this way helped people to thank those who were looking after them, feel connected to each other while they were apart, and show that they were keeping an eye on their governments' actions.

Food

Everyone needs food. It can be used to weave protest into everyday life, fuel movements, and make sure that everyone gets a more equal slice of the pie.

FREEDOM BRAIDS, 1400s-1800s

When Africans were enslaved and put on ships that would sail thousands of miles across the ocean, women found a unique way to resist. They braided rice, seeds and beans into their hair and sometimes their children's, too. When they got to the plantations in America the women planted the secret seeds so they had enough to eat and could stay connected to their culture through these familiar and nourishing foods.

REVOLUTION ON TOAST, 1960s-70s

The Black Panther movement was a radical organisation protesting systemic racism. They knew that you couldn't change the world on an empty stomach, so they set up a free breakfast program, making sure that Black children living in poverty could eat before school. The radical breakfasts quickly spread across the United States. At first the government tried to stop them but within a few years they started their own School Breakfast Program.

PEACE TEA, 1962

Friends Satish Kumar and EP Menon set out to walk from New Delhi all the way to Moscow, Paris, London and Washington, where they would meet the heads of state in charge of nuclear weapons. They hoped their 'peace pilgrimage' would inspire world leaders to think differently. When they passed a tea factory in Armenia, the women working there gave them four packets of 'peace tea'. They asked the walkers to give a packet to each leader, and to tell them, "When you think you need to press the button, stop for a minute and have a fresh cup of tea".

COTTAGE CHEESE COMRADES, 2011

Cottage cheese is one of the most popular foods in Israel, but suddenly its price almost doubled. An activist started a Facebook page calling on Israelis to stop buying cottage cheese and soon it was left to go sour on supermarket shelves. No one bought cottage cheese until the price was lowered. The unusual protest got people talking and sparked a bigger social justice movement that lowered the cost of living.

PUDDING PARTIES, 2000s

When the people of Malé in the Maldives wanted to get rid of their leader Maumoon Abdul Gayoom, how better to bring people together than with their national dish? When they organised a rice pudding party on the beach, the whole city showed up, even though mass gatherings were banned. They ate big plates of pudding and talked about how to bring down the regime. By the time police confiscated the dessert, it had already become the symbol of rebellion. Rebellious rice pudding parties were held all over the Maldives until a new leader was elected.

SIP-IN, 1966

For a long time, serving drinks to LGBTQ+ people was banned in New York City, so to draw attention to this unfair rule, a group of friends went on a bar crawl. They would tell bartenders they were gay and wait to be refused service. Proof of being discriminated against would help fight the homophobic ban. The first two bars ignored the rules and served them, which wasn't what they needed that day! But at the third bar, when the men revealed they were gay, the server stopped mid-pour. The moment was caught on camera, and the picture was splashed across the newspapers. Soon after, legally operating gay bars opened for the first time.

FOOD FUELS PROTEST, 1950s

When Georgia Gilmore was fired from her cooking job after taking part in the civil rights bus boycotts, she started a restaurant in her home in Alabama. Activists could talk and eat there in private without worrying about being overheard or even poisoned by enemies of the movement. With a group of women she also started 'The Club from Nowhere', raising money for the bus boycotts by cooking pork chops and sweet potato pies and selling them at beauty salons and churches.

Until justice rolls
down like waters

Freedom and Civil Rights

C IS FOR CONFRONTATION

Civil Rights Movement, USA, 1940s-60s

In the 1940s, many areas of life were segregated in the US, particularly in the South. This meant Black and white people were kept separate and treated differently – 80 years after the abolition of slavery, Black people still faced violence and discrimination every day.

1945

1949

1950

I paid my fare and I'm not going to move

When two women from the Army Corps refused to move for a white man, the driver hit and shouted at them. Black soldiers were some of the first to take action – they were expected to fight for America but were not treated equally back home.

Edwina and Marshall Johnson were teenagers from New Jersey, where buses weren't segregated. When they came to Montgomery, Alabama they were shocked by the laws and didn't give up their seats. They were arrested.

Black passengers were told to pay their fare and then re-enter the bus through the back door. Hilliard Brooks, another veteran back from the war, refused. The driver called the police, who beat and shot Hilliard. He died from his wounds.

One of the first places African Americans started to fight back was on the buses.
Black people were only allowed to sit at the back, and had to give up their seats
if white passengers wanted them.

1955

1955

1955

I didn't feel like I was breaking the law

Fifteen-year-old Claudette Colvin knew the segregation laws were wrong. She was arrested for refusing to move for a white woman. She recited poetry to calm herself while she was dragged away.

Claudette inspired many others to take action on the buses. Miss Sue could pass as white, but refused to and always told bus drivers they were mistaken. She sat at the front of the bus, got arrested and her case went to court, helping end segregation.

Rosa Parks had been actively fighting against racist laws for a long time. When she didn't get up from her seat, news of her arrest spread fast through Montgomery's Black community. They would come together to support Rosa and to fight back.

Rosa Parks' arrest sparked a bus boycott: Black people in Montgomery would stay off the buses. Black-owned taxi companies agreed to give people rides to work, and lots of people chose to walk in the rain rather than act as if the buses were safe or fair to ride. They walked for 13 months, until the US Supreme Court decided to end segregation on public buses.

The movement caught fire. Groups sprang up all over the south, often starting in church congregations and universities and soon the networks existed for huge protests to be organised.

In the 50s and 60s, one place teenagers loved to hang out was at the lunch counter of their local drugstore, where they could drink milkshakes, gossip and listen to the jukebox. But because of segregation, Black students were not allowed at the counter.

One day four students in Greensboro, North Carolina decided that it was time for this stupid rule to end. At 4.30pm on the 1st of February 1960, they walked up to a whites-only lunch counter, sat down and ordered coffee. Despite being threatened and yelled at, they stayed until the store closed. The next day, the students came back to the lunch counter, bringing their friends and their homework with them. Soon lunch counters in neighbouring towns were filled with young Black people refusing to leave, and within two months the sit-ins were happening in 54 different cities in nine states.

Activists were trained in peacefully standing their ground, and spent hours practising being yelled at and having ketchup poured on them. Though they knew their clothes would end up covered in condiments, they always dressed smartly for the protests. "We didn't want anyone to criticise us for our appearance because our message was controversial enough," said the activist Joan Countryman. Sometimes they wore sunglasses to hide their identities or emotions from the people watching.

By going straight to where they wanted to see change happen, the protesters made sure they couldn't be ignored, and it wasn't long before many lunch counters started serving Black customers.

Creative protests continued everywhere there was discrimination. The next summer, young Black and white activists decided they would sit together on long-distance buses. These 'Freedom Rides' angered racists so much that they firebombed one of the buses and threatened to set fire to a Black church where an emergency meeting of activists was being held. The racist attacks were so extreme that the President was pressured to send in police and army convoys to protect the protesters and get them to their destinations. Thanks to the bravery of the activists who kept joining the rides in greater and greater numbers, interstate buses became a place where Black and white passengers could sit side by side.

But there was still more to do. In 1963, Martin Luther King, Jr., one of the most inspiring leaders of the movement, travelled to Birmingham, Alabama, to launch 'Project C' for Confrontation. A new wave of nonviolent direct action was about to begin, and this time, even children would get involved. It was time for a Children's Crusade.

One Thursday morning in May, seventh grader Gwendolyn Sanders led her classmates out of school. The principal tried to stop them by locking the gates, but they climbed out of the windows, streamed past him and gathered together with hundreds of children from all over the city at a church downtown.

Using walkie-talkies to coordinate their movements, the children set off 50 at a time towards local shops, restaurants and government buildings. They would go into segregated businesses and speak to the owners about how unfair the laws were. As they marched peacefully through the streets, police began to arrest them. But more children just flowed out of the church to take their place.

By the second day of the protest, the police were running out of space in their cells. Newspapers published photographs of the children being attacked with fire hoses and called the emergency services a national disgrace. Ashamed, members of the Fire Department refused to aim their hoses at the children any more, and apologised by helping to clean up one of the churches they had flooded the day before.

When the protesters filled the streets, the shops had to shut. Within a few days business owners had agreed to the protesters' demands for integration. The cruelty of Alabama's government was exposed, the Police Commissioner was fired, the Mayor left office, and Birmingham became a different city.

What happened in Birmingham led to one of the biggest marches in America's history, when the whole civil rights movement came together to show its strength. The March on Washington for Jobs and Freedom took place that August. Whole trains and planes of activists arrived from all over the country to listen to Martin Luther King, Jr.'s famous "I have a dream" speech.

The next year the Civil Rights Act was passed, followed by further changes to voting and housing rights. The struggle for civil rights in the 1950s and 60s was one of the most effective protest movements of all time, winning drastic change and inspiring activists to this day.

GAY POWER!
The Stonewall Riots, USA, 1969

The 1960s were a very hard time to be queer in the US. LGBTQ+ people were made to feel ashamed and unwelcome almost everywhere and had to hide their identities to avoid being excluded, arrested or attacked.

People had started to protest, and at first their marches were focused on showing people the gay community could be respectable and 'normal', with protesters wearing sensible suits and dresses. They politely called these events 'Annual Reminders of Gay Rights'. But even though there had been some changes to the law, LGBTQ+ people were still treated like second-class citizens and had to live their lives in secret.

One of the only places LGBTQ+ people could be themselves were gay bars, but even these were not really safe – many were run by the mafia and regularly raided by police. The Stonewall Inn in New York City was an important gathering place. It wasn't just the only gay bar where you were allowed to dance: it also provided a sanctuary for many homeless young people who had been forced onto the streets because they were queer.

One night when police raided the Stonewall and started arresting people, they expected everyone else to leave quietly as usual. But the queer community had truly had enough. Instead of letting the raid end their night, more people arrived, surrounding the Inn and trapping the cops inside. When police reinforcements showed up, they started attacking people. It turned into a riot. Everywhere the police turned there were protesters there to meet them with colourful acts of resistance.

The riots lasted for six nights, with trans activists of colour like Marsha P. Johnson and Sylvia Rivera at the heart of the action. It's hard to know exactly what happened because the newspapers at the time didn't think queer issues were worth the ink. Little did they know that the Stonewall Riots would go down in history as one of the biggest turning points in the battle for LGBTQ+ rights.

After Stonewall, more radical organisations were formed, like the Street Transvestite Action Revolutionaries (STAR) and the Gay Liberation Front. Every year the riots are commemorated around the world with the marches and celebrations now known as Pride.

FREE SOUTH AFRICA

Anti-Apartheid Movement, South Africa, 1940s-90s

Like many other countries, South Africa was colonised by white settlers from Europe in the 17th century. Right from the beginning, anti-Black racism became part of everyday life.

When a new government came to power in 1948, this racism became law. It was called apartheid, which means separateness. Black people were forced to move to different areas away from white people. They had to leave their homes and communities, take badly paid jobs, and go to poorer schools and hospitals. The government wanted to know where Black South Africans were at all times, so they made them carry passbooks everywhere.

As the new laws made life harder for Black people and people of colour, they started thinking about how they could take back their rights. Young activists including Nelson Mandela, Oliver Tambo and Walter Sisulu were part of a new Defiance Campaign that organised many nonviolent protests. People burned their passbooks and deliberately broke apartheid laws.

If they saw whites-only signs in buses, toilets and restaurants, Defiance protesters ignored them and walked right in, just like civil rights activists were starting to do in the US. The protesters hoped that if enough of them got arrested and went to prison, the government would run out of cells and have to change the laws.

The government was determined to stop the protests at any cost, and they just squeezed more people into the jails. They put leaders like Nelson Mandela in prison for a long time to make it harder to organise the resistance. And when people did demonstrate, the police attacked them.

In 1960, thousands of people decided they would defy the laws by leaving their passbooks at home. They marched peacefully to a police station in Sharpeville expecting to be arrested. But the police began to shoot, even as the protesters ran away. Many people were killed and over the next few days, tens of thousands more were arrested all over the country.

After Sharpeville, anti-apartheid activists had to go underground or leave the country, but the tragedy had woken the world up to what was happening in South Africa. Protest groups sprang up in many different countries. They would help keep the flame alive while the South African activists were in hiding.

To support the fight against apartheid, many people around the world stopped buying South African goods. It was an easy way to send a message to the South African government that their racist policies were not acceptable.

Protesters also boycotted the whites-only South African sports teams. In the UK, rugby and cricket pitches were invaded by crowds of young people who cared about what was happening to their fellow humans thousands of miles away. Early one morning, South African players were lacing up their shoes in their hotel rooms and getting ready to leave for a match. But when they went to open their doors they couldn't turn the handles. Before anyone was awake, a girl had snuck into the hotel and glued up all the locks.

Another time, the team got on their bus – but an activist had got there first, dressed as a driver. He calmly drove the whole team to a field in the middle of nowhere, leaving them stranded at the exact moment they should have been walking onto the pitch. Protesters would do anything to stop matches from happening. They even threatened to release a family of moles onto a playing field, covering the immaculate turf with unsightly molehills.

Meanwhile, in South Africa, the movement was evolving. The new Black Consciousness Movement focused on Black pride, and the importance of Black culture and dignity beyond basic human rights.

This philosophy was behind the Soweto Uprising led by schoolchildren in 1976, when the government decided that all children would be taught in the Dutch coloniser's language of Afrikaans, and not allowed to use their native languages. Each school day usually began with the children singing the Lord's Prayer in Afrikaans, but on the day of the uprising, the pupils shocked their teachers by singing the African hymn Nkosi Sikelel' iAfrika – God Bless Africa. Not even their parents had been in on their plan. When they had finished singing, groups of pupils went from school to school gathering more children to join their strike.

Thousands and thousands of students took part. The fact that the protesters were children did not stop the police responding with brutality. The anger and sadness that erupted in the aftermath of the police violence led to the governments of other countries taking a stand against the apartheid regime, refusing to sell them weapons, lend them money, or have them at the table in important meetings.

By the 1980s, people had been fighting to end apartheid for over 30 years. They'd never seen so much support from around the world. With momentum building, activists allowed themselves to believe that South Africa might be on the brink of change at last. It was time to prepare for the end of apartheid.

Exiled activists wanted to return for the final push, but knew they would be arrested if they were recognised. They would need disguises and places to hide. Wigs, false teeth and fake noses were made and special outfits were sewn, with the help of sympathetic dentists and friends in the world of theatre. Some European activists even moved to South Africa, set up home and hired gardeners and cooks to work for them. The secret was that the gardeners and cooks were really anti-apartheid activists using the houses as offices where they could plan the end of the regime.

They ramped up their tactics and decided that if the government wasn't going to serve them, they would make South Africa ungovernable. Protests erupted on streets across South Africa. Police tried to stop protesters by spraying them with purple dye so that they could tell who had been at a protest. But being purple became something to be proud of. People started saying, "The purple shall govern!"

By this time, Nelson Mandela had been in prison for 27 years. He had become world famous for his selfless commitment to the struggle. In far-away countries, streets and buildings had been named after him. By 1990, 29 million people were boycotting South Africa. The number of people against apartheid both inside the country and around the world was so huge that the President of South Africa knew that it was the beginning of the end of the racist regime. Nelson Mandela was released from prison and four years later Black South Africans were able to vote for the first time. They elected Mandela as President.

Sports

Sports come with their own ready-made crowd and TV cameras ready to transmit whatever happens to a national or even global audience. Whether by protesting from the stands or the pitch, activists invite spectators to become both witness and participant.

PODIUM PROTEST, 1968

In 1968, a group of athletes realised the Olympics could be a stage for demanding human rights. When they won medals, sprinters Tommie Smith and John Carlos took to the podium and raised black-gloved fists in a Black Power salute. To represent Black poverty and discrimination in the USA, they wore black socks and no shoes. People booed and even threw things, but the iconic image of the protesters was broadcast onto TV screens across the world, and has become one of the most famous moments in history. "So many people find inspiration in that portrait," John Carlos said. "That's what I was born for."

STADIUM SISTERS, 1990s-

For 40 years, women had been banned from going to football matches in Iran. In 1997, 5,000 women stormed a match, shouting and waving their banners in front of the TV cameras, and avoiding arrest in the enormous crowds. More recently, smaller numbers of women have snuck in dressed as men, revealing their identities once inside. After decades of protest, in 2019, 100 Iranian women were allowed to go to a match for the first time. The struggle for all women to attend continues.

YOU CAN'T PLAY, 1960s-90s

As outrage about apartheid grew, more and more teams refused to play against South Africa. Players of many sports including table tennis, cricket, rugby and chess took a stand by not turning up to matches. This caused such disruption that soon the ruling bodies banned South Africa from participating in many sporting events, including the Olympic Games. Even when they did take part, their scores were sometimes not recorded. This was part of the many international solidarity actions supporting the end of apartheid.

MAY TYRANTS TREMBLE, 1970s-80s

When Uruguay was ruled by a tyrannical government, anyone openly protesting would be jailed. But at football matches people found a way to show how they felt. During the national anthem, people sang along as half-heartedly as possible – except for one line: "MAY TYRANTS TREMBLE". At this part of the song, the crowd went wild, singing at the top of their voices. The government didn't know what to do. Banning the line would be too embarrassing, and they couldn't punish everyone in the stadium. The collective show of resistance kept hope alive, and eventually the tyrants fell.

RESISTANCE RIDER, 1940s

During the Nazi occupation of Italy, famous cyclist Gino Bartali smuggled false identification papers and money to help Jewish people leave the country safely. He hid documents in his bike frame and handlebars, cycling long distances through the mountains between cities. He pretended he was training, and if anyone tried to inspect his bike, he told them that touching it would mess up its delicate aerodynamics. Bartali was so famous and important to Italian sport that the police would never dare arrest him. His actions saved over 800 lives, but he never spoke about it. "Some medals are made to hang on the soul, not on the jacket," he said.

TAKE A KNEE, 2016

NFL player Colin Kaepernick decided that he could no longer sing the US national anthem before games. "I am not going to stand up to show pride in a flag for a country that oppresses Black people and people of color," he said. When he began kneeling instead of singing, many football fans were outraged. Other players kept kneeling, and in 2020, taking a knee became a symbol of protest worldwide after the police killing of George Floyd. More recently, many players have protested by refusing to take part in matches altogether.

Be realistic,
demand the
impossible

FRANCE IS BORED

Student Protests, Paris, May 1968

In the 1960s, things were being shaken up all over the world, but to young French people it felt like everything exciting was happening far away. TV had arrived, and with it came news of the civil rights and anti-war movements in America. When they saw their own President on screen for the first time, they realised just how old-fashioned and out of touch he seemed.

POLITICS HAPPENS

French universities were more about rules than learning. Students had tiny rooms where they weren't allowed to discuss politics, have their boyfriends and girlfriends to stay or even change the furniture. Their professors rarely treated them like grown-ups – instead of having conversations with the students they just looked down their noses at them and scurried back to their private staff room to talk to each other. Young people were itching to break free and be heard.

A small group of students in Nanterre who called themselves the Enragés – the Angry People – started interrupting lectures at their university. They invited their fellow students to join them outside in the sun instead of staying in the stuffy classrooms. Soon hundreds wanted to be Angry People too. Together they returned to the university, stormed into the staff room, kicked out their teachers and locked the door. This was an occupation. The students had taken over and their movement had begun. Rule-breaking rage spread to other universities, and a rebellious atmosphere took over the whole of France.

TALK TO YOUR NEIGHBOUR

nmes le pouvoir

UNIVERSITE POPULAIRE

LA BEAUTÉ EST DANS LA RUE

TRAVAILLEURS UNIS

VIVE LES OCCUPATIONS

Factory workers felt they had been underpaid for a long time, so when they saw what the students were doing they seized the moment and began to strike. Others joined in and within two months, there were 10 million protesters on the streets, occupying theatres, refusing to work or go to class, and living a new way of life. Brightly-coloured revolutionary posters were screenprinted in 'art factories' and appeared everywhere, turning Paris into a gallery covered with slogans.

ON THE STREETS

With so many workers involved, it wasn't long before the whole of France had come to a standstill. No one was driving to work, so the streets were empty of cars and full of people wandering around, talking to each other and turning strangers into friends. Worried about who would take away the rubbish and stock up the shops if the workers didn't come back soon, the government offered them a big pay rise.

The protests were so powerful that the government almost lost power, and the students could have asked for anything they wanted. But that wasn't the point. They were sick of the idea that politics meant choosing sides, and were trying to create a life where they didn't have to follow anyone's rules. In this, they succeeded. The students went back to university in the autumn – but they had changed France forever. It was now more free, more fun and more rebellious. France had become a place where you could express yourself and expect to be listened to.

BE REALISTIC! DEMAND THE IMPOSSIBLE

LA LUTTE CONTINUE

MAI 68
DÉBUT D'UNE LUTTE PROLONGÉE

TREE HUGGERS
Chipko Movement, India, 1970s

The Himalayas are a mountain range covered in forests and small villages where people have lived for thousands of years. The trees have always been part of an ecosystem that keeps everything working. The leaves clean the air and the branches provide firewood, material for making farm tools, and habitats for wildlife. The roots of the trees go deep into the earth, keeping everything in place.

Things began to change when big companies realised they could chop down the trees to make money. One day there was a flood and parts of the mountain started sliding away into the river, taking houses, bridges and roads with them. The villagers knew that the roots of the trees had been holding the mountain together. They had to do something to stop the trees being cut down.

The people tried to tell the Chief Minister of the government how they felt, but it made no difference. Far away in his office in the city, he thought the villagers were just being emotional. Surely money was more important than trees! To the villagers' dismay, he ignored their wishes and sold all the trees to a big company for making into tennis racquets.

But when the woodcutters came, the villagers had got to the forest first. They banged drums and shouted until the woodcutters ran off and took their chainsaws with them.

The Chief Minister told the tennis racquet company they could have a different forest, but the people who lived in that forest weren't going to give away their trees without a fight either.

For six months the people took turns to watch over the trees day and night. Yet again the woodcutters were forced to leave.

But the tennis racquet company wanted their wood and the Chief Minister wanted money. So he looked on his map and found a third forest full of tall trees that would be perfect for making tennis racquets.

When a local girl saw the woodcutters arrive at the third forest, she ran to fetch the women of the village, who were at home doing their chores. They told her the old story of a Maharajah who had wanted wood to build a new palace. "The Maharajah sent soldiers to cut down a forest of sacred trees, but a young woman saw what was happening and put her arms around a tree trunk," they told her. "It wasn't long before the forest was full of hundreds of tree-lovers, each hugging a trunk."

The villagers wondered if the same tactic could work now? Surely the woodcutters wouldn't dare chop down a tree if someone was hugging it.

The women clung to the trees all night and became known as Chipko, which means to stick or cling in Hindi. They weren't just sticking to the trees but to their principles, too. News of their extraordinary action spread to the neighbouring villages and soon more tree huggers arrived to help. The woodcutters gave up.

It wasn't long before the Chief Minister heard about what was going on. If things carried on this way the tennis racquets would never be made – but maybe tennis racquets weren't so important after all. The government banned all tree cutting in the Himalayas, until the mountains were green again.

HANDS AROUND THE BASE
Greenham Common Peace Camp, UK, 1981-2000

It was the middle of the Cold War, an ideological battle between the communist-led Soviet Union and the capitalist United States, and both sides were stockpiling nuclear weapons. When Britain saw how many nuclear weapons everyone else had, it wanted to get more of its own.

A group of women in Wales were worried – nuclear war would have disastrous consequences for humanity. They waited for someone else to organise a protest to sort the problem out. But when no one did, they realised they would have to do it themselves.

Many of them had never protested before. They didn't know what to do, only that they had to do something. First they came up with a name: Women for Life on Earth. Then they made leaflets. The plan was to walk the hundreds of miles to the base at Greenham Common, where the weapons were being stored. Surely that would be enough to get the government's attention.

The walk to Greenham was one of the most adventurous things many of them had ever done. But after days of walking, it was obvious that no one else was interested – and the only thing on the news was a pregnant panda who was about to give birth. The women would have to up the ante. Inspired by the Suffragettes, they decided that when they arrived, they would chain themselves to the fence.

Now people were interested. The police arrived and started cutting their chains off, but each time a woman got carted away, another was always there to take her place. Others slept nearby to support the locked-on women, bringing tents and making fires to keep themselves warm. Soon the base was surrounded by tents as word spread around the country. They had replaced the panda on the front pages of the newspapers and all the publicity brought more and more women to Greenham. By the following winter there were enough protesters to join hands around the entire base.

With the camp set up, the women could take action almost every day. They found many different ways to get through the fence surrounding the missiles, cutting into bits of it, or putting scraps of carpet over the barbed wire so they could climb over safely. When they got inside they danced on the missile trucks and stopped them from leaving by sticking potatoes in the exhaust pipes. They had made an art out of being annoying, ready to thwart the authorities at every turn.

In 1987 a treaty was signed banning many nuclear weapons, and in 1991 the last missiles left the base at Greenham Common. The protesters had won. Everyone expected them to go home, but they weren't in the business of living up to other people's expectations. Some went on to become prominent politicians, journalists and professors. Others stayed at the camp for another nine years campaigning for peace. Eventually the Common became a public park where people could walk their dogs and play with their children.

Camping

Whether in a tent or a tree, camping means you can get to the heart of the action, right up close to the thing you want to protect or protest. By camping together, protesters have also created communities which put their beliefs into practice.

PUREORA TREE-SITTERS, 1978

A group of activists and conservationists wanted to save the 1000-year-old podocarp trees of a New Zealand forest from logging. They tried petitions and scientific reports, but it was only when they camped in high platforms built into the branches that the loggers stopped. The sitters stayed for four days until the government agreed to put a permanent end to all logging. Pureora inspired activists all over the world to save trees by sitting in them.

LUNA THE REDWOOD TREE, 1997-99

Julia Butterfly Hill was 23 when she started sitting in an 1000-year-old Redwood tree which was threatened by logging in Humboldt County, California. She stayed there for 738 days (more than two years!), sleeping on a small platform 55 metres up in the air. She was supported by a group of people who took turns to hoist food and supplies to her. She let her feet get dirty, which helped them stick to the branches better. The tree and the surrounding grove were saved.

CLIMATE CAMP, 2006-10

Each summer for five years, tents popped up at airports, power stations and in the City of London, creating a base for direct action stunts aimed at stopping carbon emissions from those places. The camps, which ran on solar and wind power and had pedal-powered laundries and sound systems, gave people the opportunity to create communities of resistance while living in a low-carbon way.

WHITE HOUSE PEACE VIGIL, 1981-2016

Pacifist William Thomas camped outside the White House for 27 years to protest the USA's nuclear weapons programme. He met Ellen Benjamin when she joined the protest in 1984. They fell in love, got married and lived there permanently with their dog Sophie, friend Connie and different groups who came to support them, including the Occupy and Plowshares movements. Their presence inspired the introduction of a nuclear disarmament act to Congress and was a constant reminder of opposition to war.

OCCUPY, 2011

Occupy was a worldwide movement against social and economic inequality that began in response to the global financial crisis, when banks were receiving more government support than people were. A camp with the slogan "We are the 99%" popped up overnight in Wall Street, the heart of New York's financial district. Within a month, there were camps in 951 cities in 82 countries. The camps were a place to practise participatory democracy, share ideas and amplify the voice of a generation that had been let down by capitalism's broken promises.

OCCUPATION OF ALCATRAZ, 1969-71

When the prison island of Alcatraz, off the coast of San Francisco, was shut down, Native Americans sailed there to reclaim the Indigenous land which had been promised to them under the Treaty of Fort Laramie. Families lived there in tents and in the old prison, staying for 18 months. Their occupation resulted in new laws supporting Native People and the return of thousands of acres of Native land across America.

POOR PEOPLE'S CAMP-IN, 1967-68

After the early successes of the civil rights movement, Martin Luther King, Jr. wanted to expand the campaign's demands to include rights to food and shelter for all poor Americans. Three thousand protesters travelled to Washington, D.C., and camped on the Washington Mall near the White House for six weeks, building temporary houses complete with electricity and running water. They called it Resurrection City. Passing them every day on their way to work, the politicians could no longer ignore them.

Freedom for those who think differently

People Power Revolutions

SOLIDARITY!

Solidarność Movement, Poland, 1980-89

After the Second World War, many countries in Eastern Europe had new governments. Their new systems of keeping law and order (or 'regimes' as they are often called) were known for their strict rules and nosiness about their citizens' lives, controlling and watching everything they did. Although protest wasn't allowed, people found creative ways to resist.

The television news was full of propaganda about how great the regime was, how happy and well-paid the workers were and how there weren't any problems. Eventually, a workers' union called Solidarność (Polish for 'solidarity') had enough of this and switched off their TVs. But what was the point if nobody knew that they weren't watching? So they put their unplugged TVs on their windowsills, facing outwards. Maybe this would inspire other people to turn off too, until the government had no one left to lie to.

They sat inside with their TVs on the windowsills and stared at the wallpaper. Solidarność knew they were doing the right thing, but it was a bit boring. They might as well be outside, enjoying their neighbours' company. Before long the streets were full of people strolling around during the evening news, pushing their TVs along in wheelbarrows. The government was angry that their elaborate lies were going to waste, so they imposed a curfew: it was now illegal to be outside after 7pm. The citizens didn't care – they just took their TVs out during the 5 o'clock news instead.

Then the citizens had another idea – they would make their own news. Radio Solidarity was born. The underground radio station could be broadcast anonymously and was a very important tool for telling the truth and organising the resistance. The radio was also used as a way for the people to show that they were unified against the regime. The radio host would ask people to turn their lights on and off at certain points in the programme, and all over Poland the sight of blinking lights flashing from windows gave people hope.

As the members of Solidarność realised just how many of them there were, they wanted to do bigger and bolder things. This was difficult when the government was so strict about anything that looked like a protest. What if, instead of a protest, they did the opposite?

The regime had planned a big celebration of itself, to show the world how brilliantly it was ruling Poland. For the protesters, it was the perfect opportunity to show they didn't agree. On the big day, thousands of people arrived dressed top to toe in bright red (the regime's favourite colour) and people who didn't have any red clothes bought baguettes, covered them in ketchup and waved them around like flags. They were so over the top in their enthusiasm that it was clear they were making a mockery of the whole thing. There was not much the police could do – how could they arrest people for supporting the government so passionately?

Over the next 10 years, hundreds of these actions weakened the authority of the regime. In 1989 free elections were held for the first time since before the Second World War. The leader of Solidarność, Lech Wałęsa, became President of Poland, and the regime ended peacefully.

OUR DIGNITY IS NOT NEGOTIABLE
People Power Revolution, Philippines, 1986

By 1986 the Philippines had been ruled by the dictator Ferdinand Marcos for over 20 years. Ferdinand seemed to spend more time making movies about himself than governing the country, and his wife Imelda was always spending public money on big fancy buildings, shoes and handbags.

As their rulers got richer, the Filipino people got poorer. They tried to get rid of Marcos in lots of different ways, but their sit-ins, strikes and demonstrations never worked. Their movement needed a leader to run against Marcos in the elections and take back power for the people. A man called Benigno Aquino, Jr. put himself forward. He was a popular candidate and it looked like he stood a good chance. But to everyone's horror, he was assassinated before the elections.

Aquino's wife Cory was heartbroken, but when she saw two million people join her husband's funeral procession, she realised how powerful people could be when they came together. At that moment she knew she had to unite the country in opposition.

Cory's passion for the Filipino people was infectious. Soon all parts of society were trying to bring Ferdinand Marcos down. When Benigno died, mourners wore yellow ribbons to the funeral, and yellow quickly became the colour of the protests. The business district held weekly confetti demonstrations, scattering shredded yellow phone books from their office windows. Thousands of farmers came to the city and sat in front of the Ministry of Agriculture for days and days. And half a million people ran the length of three marathons between the Aquinos' house and the airport where Benigno was assassinated – showing their dedication to democracy.

Marcos was rattled. Still living in a fantasy land, he called an election to prove how much the people enjoyed living under his dictatorship. But his plan backfired when a million people signed a letter urging Cory Aquino to stand for President. Now Marcos was even more worried. He told all the vote counters to rub out all the votes for Cory, and change them into votes for him. But they refused to obey, and walked out.

It was time for the People Power Revolution. The elections started an avalanche of disobedience. No longer scared of him, hundreds of Marcos' soldiers switched sides. Instead of walking around with guns intimidating people into following his rules, they stayed in their military camps. Thousands of Filipinos came to support them, bringing food and singing songs. They protected the rebellious troops by blocking the roads with tree trunks and buses that were parked sideways.

When Marcos sent in more soldiers, the brave protesters gave the tank drivers flowers, chocolates and hamburgers. Their kindness inspired the tank drivers to join the revolution. No one was hurt, and Cory went out to the people to declare her victory as the new leader of the Philippines.

Ferdinand and Imelda left for Hawaii. They never publicly admitted that they had lost power – but they never came back.

WHO WILL SHOUT IF NOT US?

Tiananmen Square, China, 1989

Chairman Mao ruled China as a dictatorship for 27 years. While he was in power he caused the deaths of millions of Chinese people through torture and starvation. After he died in 1976, everyone breathed a sigh of relief. At last the big posters of his face would come down off the walls and maybe the country would become a nicer place to live.

The new generation had fresh ideas and hope for the future. A group of students decided to present their suggestions to the government. But every time they knocked on the door of the Great Hall of the People, they were turned away. Instead of speaking with them, the leader of the government wrote an article on the front page of The People's Daily newspaper, telling everyone that the students were dangerous enemies of China who were causing chaos and starting riots.

When they read these lies about themselves, the peaceful students marched to Tiananmen Square in the centre of Beijing. The police looked on, confused by the procession of smiling, singing protesters who were so different from the ruffians described by the government. The police went home but the students stayed. They set up camp.

More and more students came to Tiananmen Square every day, but the government still didn't listen. The students had to do more. They began a hunger strike, refusing to eat or leave until their demands were met. People all over China watched the starving students on the news and felt moved by their passion.

Meanwhile, Mikhail Gorbachev, the leader of the Soviet Union, was about to visit. The Chinese government wanted to impress him. They needed to make everything and everyone look clean, tidy and obedient before he arrived. But the students in the Square had been joined by people from all over China and the protests were getting bigger and more embarrassing by the minute. When Gorbachev arrived, he was kept away from the Square with a hasty handshake at the airport.

The government was fuming and sent in the army. To the soldiers' surprise, when they arrived at the Square, the students asked them how they were and gave them flowers. The protesters reminded them that they were the People's Army. 'Yes, we're here to protect the people!' the soldiers thought, and left without carrying out their orders.

To make matters worse for the government, a million Beijing workers went on strike in solidarity with the students. A mass movement like this was unheard of in China's repressive regime. None of the protesters had ever lived in a democratic state like the one that was being born in Tiananmen Square. The people governed themselves with kindness and consideration, voting every night on whether to leave or stay (they always chose to stay). All kinds of Beijingers supported the students – thieves even put up posters announcing that they would stop stealing during the protests.

The government couldn't bear watching this vision of an alternative China come to life, and the party leader went off to find new soldiers. Once the new army was ready, they made an announcement: the Square would be cleared that night.

As darkness fell, Beijingers flocked to the Square to protect the students they had come to love and admire so much. They tried to build barricades to keep out the tanks. But the new army was too powerful. That night, many of the protesters lost their lives.

Two days later, as the tanks rolled through the empty square, a solitary man appeared out of nowhere and calmly walked in front of them. For a few long minutes he faced off with the tank at the front of the line, with nothing but his bags of groceries to protect him. Each time the tank steered away from him, he moved to stay in its path. This final act of bravery symbolised the Chinese people's struggle and created one of the most famous images of protest ever seen.

WE WANT OUT! WE WANT IN!
Fall of the Berlin Wall, Germany, 1989

One August night in 1961, the government of East Germany started to build a wall across Berlin. The next morning people woke up to find their families split apart, and friends living on opposite sides of the wall didn't know if they would ever see each other again. The government told their citizens that the wall would keep out the dangers of the West. On the other side, they said, people got up to no good, spent all their money on jeans and watched too much TV. But mostly the wall just stopped East Germans from leaving.

A few brave escapees tried to leave by hot air balloon, secret tunnels or ziplines. A trapeze artist even tightrope-walked along a disused power cable! Not only were the escape methods often dangerous, but if you didn't succeed, you risked severe punishment in prison.

It was hard to plan anything without being found out. East Germans were not only controlled by the wall but also by an enormous secret police force called the Stasi, who made sure that everyone was following the rules and not getting any funny ideas. Phone calls were snooped on, people were followed, and even telling a joke that made fun of the government could get you arrested.

There were so many Stasi that it was likely most people had spies among their friends and family, who made notes on everything they did and said. It was hard to trust anyone, so when people started to protest they had to go undercover. Rebellious ideas spread through underground newsletters and secret parties in people's back gardens.

At the local elections in 1989, the government announced it had won, as it always did. But this time activists had been outside the polling stations, asking people who they'd really

voted for. They got their calculators out and proved that more people had voted against the government than for it. Now the government's lies had been exposed, the East Germans were more determined than ever to tear down the wall. Thousands of people started marching on the streets, and soon protests were happening all over the country, every day.

With the protests on the news around the world, the leader of East Germany was forced to resign. The unthinkable had happened. Despite the strictest police force in the world, the people had still managed to take back power from under the government's nose.

Desperate to get the people on their side, the government had an idea. They made an announcement that East Germans would be allowed to go on holiday – but only if they came straight back! It didn't work. Instead of booking their holidays through the official travel bureau, tens of thousands of people rushed to the wall. The crowds overwhelmed the surprised guards, who had no choice but to let them through to the other side, where they were reunited with their old friends, and started pulling down the wall together, for good.

Within weeks, citizens were occupying Stasi offices to reclaim their secret files. And soon the Stasi themselves were challenging the government, joining in with their own top-secret demonstration behind the walls of the Ministry of Security.

Without their police, the Government could no longer resist the new spirit of the country, and within a year there was no East or West – just Germany, reunified at last.

Art

Creativity is at the heart of protest, and artists have always found new ways to disrupt the order of things. Using an array of techniques from performance to painting, artist-activists have inspired people to see the world differently.

TACTICS

PRINTS FOR THE PEOPLE, 1400s

As soon as printing was invented, it became useful as a tool for protest. Pictures could be used to spread messages to the large numbers of people who had not been taught to read. Many prints showed the powerful behaving badly. Whether the drawings were angry or funny, they were eagerly bought from travelling printsellers and shared between friends, getting everyone talking.

CREATIVE COMPLAINING, 1980s-

Black feminist artist Lorraine O'Grady was sick of not being invited to take part in exhibitions. She turned up at art openings dressed as her alter ego Mademoiselle Bourgeoise Noire and loudly recited poems about the exclusion of Black artists. Around the same time, the Guerrilla Girls started donning gorilla masks to do undercover 'creative complaining', exposing discrimination with challengeing posters. Their most famous one asked "Do Women Have to be Naked to Get into the Met. Museum?" because that museum featured more paintings of nude women than paintings by women artists.

BANNERS, 1800s-

Banners are a common sight at protests today, but they only became popular fairly recently in the 19th century. They emerged as a way for trade unions to display their symbols and were soon used at marches for workers' rights. The banners were beautifully designed, often by British artist George Tutill, who invented a technique of painting on silk widely copied for the next 150 years. Later, the Artists' Suffrage League were another big influence on the craft, hand-embroidering hundreds of banners for the many suffragette processions.

GUERNICA, 1937

When the Spanish village of Guernica was destroyed by Nazi bombers, Pablo Picasso painted what happened and displayed the picture at the Paris World Fair. Next it toured the world, raising money and awareness for those resisting the fascists in Spain's civil war. For a long time the painting hung in New York's Museum of Modern Art, where protesters held anti-war vigils in front of it. A tapestry version hangs at the United Nations, but was covered up when Secretary of State Colin Powell stood in front of it in 2003 to explain why the USA should invade Iraq. The powerful image might have reminded people that peace is better than war.

THE WALLS ARE ALIVE, 1930s

Murals – paintings on walls instead of canvases – have been used by many artists as a way to get their work seen without needing the approval of art galleries. One of the most famous political muralists was Diego Rivera, who made murals about Mexico so that its history could be understood by everyone, even people who couldn't read. His vision of a different world for workers inspired US President Roosevelt to start a New Deal which put ordinary people first.

GAY WEDDING, 1968

Japanese artist Yayoi Kusama describes one of her artworks as the first gay wedding in the United States. She held it in her own home and arranged all the details as she would with one of her intricate paintings, including the clothing. The couple wore a wedding dress made for two instead of one: "Clothes ought to bring people together," she said. She protested by using art to show things that were usually hidden or forbidden.

DARKER COLOURS, 1960s

Faith Ringgold is a Black artist, feminist and activist who has thought deeply about using materials politically. In the 60s, she noticed that many white western artists used a lot of white paint and centred their compositions around the contrast between dark and light. As a protest against the way that white artists often see the world through the lens of their skin tone, she began to work in a style common in African art, using darker paint and more colours.

Another world
is possible

Acting Up, Speaking Out

ACT UP
AIDS Coalition to Unleash Power, USA, 1980s-90s

In the 1980s gay people noticed that a mysterious new disease was killing lots of their friends, but nobody else seemed to be talking about it. The disease was called AIDS (acquired immune deficiency syndrome), but the President of the United States refused to say its name in public for several years. It was already difficult to be gay, but when the gay community saw how little the world seemed to care, they knew their lives weren't valued as much as other people's. Even though you couldn't get the disease from doing things like sharing an office or a house, people with AIDS were often fired from their jobs and evicted from their homes.

By the end of 1986 over 25,000 people had already died in the US. Scientists were finally developing medicine to treat the disease, but it was so expensive that hardly anyone could afford it. Something needed to change. The next spring a man named Larry Kramer suggested creating a protest group to take direct action: AIDS Coalition to Unleash Power, or ACT UP.

In their first action, 250 activists descended on Wall Street, the heart of New York's financial district. To protest the big drug companies that were making money from AIDS medicine, the activists blocked traffic by lying down in the road and holding up cardboard gravestones. It was spectacular and risky, but just a small taste of what was to come.

Week after week, month after month, they kept taking action, not just in New York, but all around the USA, where ACT UP groups formed in different states. The movement included people who'd never been involved in protests before, as well as those who'd been activists for decades. A group of older lesbians brought useful skills that they had learned during the anti-war campaigns of the 1970s. But inexperience was also one of the strengths of the movement – ACT UP invented new forms of protest and didn't have time for rallies, long speeches and marches. The issue was urgent and there was no time to waste.

Sneaking into buildings was one of ACT UP's specialities. One cold January evening some protesters snuck into a TV station headquarters by dressing in business suits so boring that they blended in with everyone else going to work. They surprised the entire country by

leaping in front of the cameras during the evening news, drowning out the presenter with chants about fighting AIDS, not wars. They had shown the TV stations what a real news story looked like.

After ACT UP protesters infiltrated the Food and Drug Administration (FDA) headquarters they sent out memos on official FDA notepaper, announcing the made-up good news that AIDS medicine was now cheaper and accessible to all. The next year, they shut down the entire trading floor of the New York Stock Exchange, disrupting business for the big drug companies. Just a few days later, the price of AIDS medicine was lowered by a third.

ACT UP didn't stop there. It was their mission to understand AIDS and end the crisis for good. Some activists became experts in the science. They kept going until treatments were improved, AIDS could be talked about out loud, and millions of lives were saved. The group who had once been shunned as victims had become one of the most powerful forces in the history of protest.

FREEDOM STREET
Palestinian Resistance, Palestine, 2002-

The region of Israel-Palestine has long been contested by two groups of people who live there: the Israelis and the Palestinians. Over decades of wars, the state of Israel has taken over more and more of the land, and millions of Palestinians have been forced to leave their homes.

As well as fighting in the wars, the Palestinians also resisted nonviolently with protest. They tried boycotts, marches and strikes, and even protested by using 'Palestinian time' – putting their clocks forward a week earlier than the Israelis in spring. But eventually, in 2002, Israel began building a towering fence to separate the Israelis from the Palestinians.

The fence didn't care if you lived on one side and worked on the other. It didn't care if you had to go the long way round to get to school or go to the doctor. It didn't care if it went through the middle of a field of olive trees. But the Palestinian people cared.

From the moment construction began, the Palestinians tried to stop it.

By day, the builders knocked poles into the ground and rolled out barbed wire, and by night the Palestinians pulled it down again. As time went on the fence became more like a wall, and harder to demolish.

To claim the land and make it feel like home, the Palestinians planted olive trees and gardens next to the wall.

Artists snuck out at night to cover it with graffiti. In the early days of the wall, before smart phones and social media, the painted messages were an important way of communicating and passing on information about meetings and demonstrations. Using the green, red, white and black of the Palestinian flag they painted all sorts of things, from giant house keys and peace signs, to slogans like "Viva Palestina". But the artists were always wary of making the wall look beautiful, because they wanted people to understand that what it stood for was ugly.

As the wall grew, the protests grew too. When it wound its way through Bil'in, splitting the village in half, the villagers took the Israeli government to court to force them to change the route of the wall. The village was so small and the Israeli government was so big, that no one thought they could win – but they did. The judge ordered that the wall had to go around the outside of their village instead of cutting through the middle of it.

Of course, what the villagers really wanted was no wall at all. The road leading to the wall at Bil'in has been renamed Freedom Street, and today the villagers come together every Friday to march along it to the border. This ongoing protest has become so well known that activists from all around the world come to join in. Protesters even come from Israel – standing in solidarity with the Palestinian people. Members of Ta'ayush (the Arab-Israeli Partnership) provide practical support like making sure Palestinians can plough their fields, and helping Palestinian children get to school.

All over Palestine people continue to take action, growing a garden of resistance in the shadow of the wall. Palestinians use the Arabic word 'sumud' to describe their steadfastness and commitment to the long struggle for freedom.

THIS IS WHAT DEMOCRACY LOOKS LIKE
Battle of Seattle, USA, 1999

The world's richest nations had hired out the biggest conference centre in Seattle, where they were planning a huge meeting to talk about how they could make it easier to do trade deals between countries. The problem was that they wanted to do this by removing lots of the rules that protected workers' rights and the planet's resources. They were called the World Trade Organisation (WTO), but some people nicknamed them the World Take Over.

When they heard about the conference, activists everywhere decided it was time to get together and make this the worst WTO meeting ever. They were worried that if this tiny group of people in suits tore up the rule book, workers and the environment would pay the price. The internet, which was only a few years old, meant that for the first time activists in different countries could easily communicate with each other about standing up for their rights. They learned how their struggles were related and how much they had in common. The fight for fairer wages in India was connected to struggles to save forests in Canada, which were connected to fisherfolk losing their livelihoods to big trawlers on the world's oceans.

Together, the activists came up with lots of creative ideas about how they could use the WTO meeting to draw attention to the problems of capitalism. The week before the meeting, activists began arriving from all over the world to start putting their plans into action. They had designed a front page that looked exactly like Seattle's most popular newspaper, and began sneaking copies of it onto newsstands. Their made-up newspaper was full of stories describing the world they hoped for, where people and the planet were more important than money. But this was just the start. Soon they would be hitting the headlines for real.

Before sunrise on the first day of the meeting, activists used bike locks and handcuffs to create human chains, blocking off traffic junctions around the city. While the WTO were inside their hotels finishing their morning croissants, thousands more protesters were marching towards the conference centre from every direction.

Swinging their briefcases on the way to the meeting, the WTO had no idea what was in store for them. Suddenly they couldn't get any further. The way was blocked by students, grandparents, trade union members, environmentalists, human rights activists, marching bands, puppets, and people dressed as the animals they wanted to protect. The WTO decided to give up and come back the next day.

Eventually, after many delays, the meeting began. But, as the conference continued, so did the protests. The activists stayed all week, with giant parties erupting before dawn every day. The streets were full of joy, with people dancing, drumming, cheerleading, teaching classes, putting up banners and performing plays.

The carnival made it impossible for the meeting to carry on as normal. As the people inside shuffled their papers and tried to concentrate, their words were drowned out by the hullabaloo coming from outside. The talks were forced to end early. For a moment, the world remembered money wasn't everything. On the streets of Seattle, powerful friendships were formed between different groups who have been working together ever since.

Theatre

TACTICS

Theatre can retell the story of the world, opening up possibilities and igniting the imagination. Actor-vists have disrupted traditional performances and staged their own, using theatrical props to create spectacular imagery.

YES MEN, 2004

American duo the Yes Men use their acting skills, sense of humour and strait-laced appearance to impersonate politicians and businessmen. One of them convinced the BBC that he was a boss at the company thought to be responsible for a terrible chemical explosion in Bhopal, India. Live on the news the fake character Jude Finisterra apologised on behalf of the company, promising to pay victims' medical bills and give money to their families. The company's stock immediately plummeted. When the hoax was revealed and it emerged that the company didn't intend to help the victims after all, the world's attention was drawn to Bhopal's demands for justice.

SARCASTIC CLAPPING, 2011

People are expected to praise everything dictators do, whether they feel like it or not. In Belarus, after President Lukashenko claimed he had won yet another election, the people turned this performance of false praise into a protest, getting together in large groups to clap at nothing. The sarcastic applause annoyed the President more than if no one had clapped at all. Eventually even his supporters were scared to applaud him.

GLITTER BOMB, 2010s

When US politician Newt Gingrich said he was against gay marriage, the activist Nick Espinosa stood in line waiting to meet him at a book signing. When Espinosa got to the front of the queue, he let loose a blizzard of glitter which covered Gingrich from head to toe. "Stop the hate" and "feel the rainbow," he shouted. Other LGBTQ+ activists started using the same technique, and a year later Gingrich started trying to convince his party to support gay marriage.

WE ARE STEPPING OUT OF OUR ROLES, 1989

As the movement to pull down the Berlin Wall escalated, actors decided to speak out. At a theatre in Dresden, the cast stayed on stage at the end of their performance and declared they were "stepping out of their roles". The actors criticised the regime and invited the audience to join them in casting off the role of obedient citizen. The whole theatre company acted together, knowing that there were too many of them to arrest. When making political statements was banned, the actors simply stood on stage in silent protest. Soon actors were taking a stand all over Germany.

REHEARSAL FOR THE REVOLUTION, 1970s

Augusto Boal was a theatre director who lived in Brazil during a military dictatorship. He used his skills to invent a new kind of protest theatre. Forum theatre, which Boal called a 'rehearsal for the revolution', invites the audience to make suggestions and even join the performance. Together the actors and 'spect-actors' experiment with different ways of stopping the oppression they are experiencing in real life, so that when the curtain comes down they are ready to take action. Boal became a city councillor, using theatre to help citizens create new laws.

ACTOR-VISM, 2010s

A group called BP or not BP have protested oil company sponsorship of museums and theatres with lots of creative disruptions. They started by interrupting Shakespeare plays, jumping on stage to act out alternative scenes about the role oil companies have played in the climate crisis. Since then the actor-vists have staged over 50 performances, even invading the British Museum with a huge Viking ship and a four-metre-tall Trojan Horse. In 2019, as more people got involved in protests against fossil fuel companies, the Royal Shakespeare Company cancelled its sponsorship deal with oil company BP.

Be like water

Mubarak: Go!
My arms are tired

TURN OFF THE INTERNET!
Arab Spring, Cairo, 2011

For almost 30 years, Egypt had been ruled by a dictator called Hosni Mubarak. Many Egyptians didn't like him and he knew it. He hired more and more bodyguards to protect him and even to spy on his citizens. Then an election was called, and the people finally had a chance to get rid of him. But the election was just for show. Voters were intimidated into staying home, or voting for Mubarak, and he won again. It seemed like they would never see the back of him.

But there was hope. In neighbouring Tunisia, a people-powered revolution had turned the country upside down, and activists in Egypt had secretly been planning something similar. If there was ever going to be a good time to put their ideas into action, it was now.

They chose the date and put the event on Facebook. As the day grew nearer, the event page was visited by thousands of people a minute, all promising they would come. But no one knew if they would be able to translate this virtual protest to the real streets of Cairo, where gatherings of more than two people were banned. They would have to be clever in order to get away with it.

The official meeting place was downtown, but on the morning of the protest, the organisers set off towards the slums instead, where they would find more people to join them. By heading off in a different direction to the one they'd publicised, they confused the police and had time to gather a huge crowd. When the protesters finally arrived at Tahrir Square in the middle of Cairo, there were enough of them to stand their ground. The protesters swiftly set up a tent city, which became their home and a base for more spontaneous protests that moved fluidly around the streets and bridges of Cairo.

President Mubarak knew that this was a revolution that had started on the internet. He thought that if he switched the internet off, he could switch the revolution off too. But the Square had become an extraordinary place, a real life network of people talking and planning freely with less fear. Turning off the internet would not change that.

Soon the protest swelled to a million people. Mubarak couldn't pretend that anyone would vote for him now. After the protesters had occupied the square for 18 days, he resigned and didn't even get to give a farewell speech. The people had heard enough.

Without violence, the Egyptian people had achieved an unthinkable thing in just a few days. And this was just the beginning: protests erupted across the region in the neighbouring countries of Yemen, Bahrain, Libya, Syria, Iran and Morocco, in what became known as the Arab Spring. Everywhere you looked, another ruler was falling off his perch.

The protesters in Egypt were so focused on removing Mubarak that they didn't have time for planning what would come after, and their vision of a new society didn't become a reality. But the people will never forget what it was like living and dreaming in Tahrir Square. They proved that people-power can topple governments, bring communities together, and can end seemingly endless regimes.

DISOBEDIENT DOLLS
Toys Protest, Global, 2010s

In Russia, the only way people were allowed to protest against the regime was if they had a permit – and permits were rarely given.

In 2012, the people of a small town in Siberia found a creative way to get around the ban. They couldn't protest, but what if they sent someone or something in their place? One snowy winter's day hundreds of teddy bears, Lego people and toy soldiers appeared in Barnaul's town square holding placards and banners protesting the regime.

It wasn't long before police arrived on the scene and started noting down the slogans. The officers scratched their heads, wondering how to arrest a load of dolls. When photos of the ridiculous scene were shared all over Russia, they inspired a wave of toy protests across the whole country. The authorities knew that the people were making fun of them and they declared public gatherings of inanimate objects officially against the law.

Russia isn't the only place toys have played their part in protests.

In 2018 gatherings were banned in Krajina Square, in the Bosnian and Herzegovinian city of Banja Luka. The next year, a 'Protest without People' appeared. "Enough of you toying with us!" read one of the banners held up by stuffed elephants and teddy bears. "You can buy us in toy shops, not in elections," was written on another. Once again, the sight of police officers looming over the tiny scene made it clear just how worried the government were about anyone criticising them, even cuddly toys.

The Chinese dissident artist Ai Weiwei decided toys would make good material for his protest art when he was making portraits of political prisoners in 2014. Their photos online were often pixelated and blocky, almost like they were made up of Lego bricks.

I'm afraid I'm going to have to take your names and addresses

Once Ai had run out of his son's supply of bricks, he got in touch with the Lego factory in Denmark to ask them to send him some more. To his surprise they refused to sell him any. Instead, a letter arrived, explaining that as Ai's art was usually so political, letting him play with the toys might imply that Lego agreed with whatever subversive statement he was making. And as a politically neutral company, they couldn't have that.

But it turned out he didn't need Lego to supply him with bricks – hundreds of thousands of tiny Lego bricks started pouring in from toy boxes all around the world when Ai's fans and supporters heard about the ban. The company soon apologised, and Ai has been making portraits with the donated Lego ever since.

FLOWING IN THE STREETS
Pro-Democracy Protests, Hong Kong, 2014-

On a map Hong Kong looks like it is part of China, but for over 150 years it was ruled by Britain. So when Britain agreed to hand control of the city back to China, some Hong Kongers were worried about what this would mean. Why couldn't they rule themselves?

At first nothing much changed, but gradually laws became stricter and people had less freedom to express themselves. Young people were especially concerned. They didn't see a future for themselves in the city Hong Kong was becoming.

They tried protesting. In 2014 they occupied the streets for 79 days, but even though they brought the city to a standstill, nothing changed. Then a new rule came in, which meant that people who broke the law could be given harsher punishments. The protesters knew they had to try again. This time they came back stronger, with a fresh wave of tactics.

Their slogan was "Be Water". Martial arts star Bruce Lee had a saying – "Be like water making its way through cracks. Do not be assertive, but adjust to the object, and you shall find a way around or through it... Now, water can flow, or it can crash. Be water, my friend." For the groups of protesters, this meant being able to change their shape, flowing in and out of streets, being in many places at once and reversing direction unexpectedly.

Instead of advertising times and places in advance, the protesters used their phones to gather and disperse crowds at a moment's notice. All of these tactics confused the police and kept the protesters safe. Like water, they moved fluidly.

Teamwork was one of their best tactics. They created a sign language using arm signals, so that they could ask each other for things like helmets, marker pens and tools. The supplies travelled along human chains, sometimes hundreds of people long. Umbrellas could be seen floating through crowds, making their way to the front to shield protesters from police attacks and keep their faces hidden from cameras.

The young people inspired others to act. In a general strike, 350,000 workers came out to demand change. And at "silver-haired" protests grandparents joined their grandchildren, who taught them the hand signals while they shared snacks and stories about resistance.

The protesters were so persistent that eventually the law they were fighting was withdrawn. But they kept going, calling for democracy and independence, still being water, still flowing.

THIS STOPS HERE
Black Lives Matter, Global, 2013-

In 2013 three American women, Alicia Garza, Patrisse Cullors and Opal Tometi, set up Black Lives Matter (BLM) in response to racism and police violence against Black people in the United States.

The movement began as a hashtag after the killing of Black teenager Trayvon Martin, giving people a space to share their grief and anger, and drawing attention to how laws in the USA don't deliver justice to the victims of racist hate crimes.

Soon the online protest moved to the streets. BLM protesters took action by holding die-ins, blocking interstates and shutting down airport terminals. They developed ways of communicating and building networks so they could move quickly and mobilise large numbers of protesters in different cities at the same time.

In 2020, Black Americans were reeling from the police killings of Ahmaud Arbery and Breonna Taylor. At the same time, a disproportionate number of Black people were dying from the Covid-19 virus. When police killed another Black person, George Floyd, a new wave of BLM protests erupted all over the country, and within days, all over the world.

Protesters and mourners visited the intersection near where George Floyd died, filled it with flowers, and spray-painted the crosswalks with slogans. Soon people were pouring onto the streets in solidarity and grief all across the country.

Demonstrations lasted for weeks, calling for an end to the racist systems that had caused the deaths of so many Black people. The protesters wanted governments to give less money to the police and invest in communities instead. Some activists created 'autonomous zones', collections of streets and parks where police were kept out so that the protesters could plan their next actions.

Seattle's Capitol Hill Autonomous Zone lasted almost a month, long enough for protesters to plant a vegetable garden, set up a food co-op and paint the words 'Black Lives Matter' on the road, so big they stretched the length of a whole block.

In Bristol in the UK, BLM protesters surprised everyone by using ropes to pull down a statue of 17th century slave trader Edward Colston. After they had toppled the heavy bronze figure from its plinth, they rolled it along the road and threw it into the sea. Afterwards they taped up a cardboard sign that read, "This plaque is dedicated to the slaves that were taken from their homes". Since then monuments all over the world that glorify figures linked to colonialism and the slave trade have been defaced, decapitated, spray-painted or removed. Many city councils have taken down statues themselves as the BLM movement continues to raise awareness of the problems with celebrating historical figures who have caused so much pain.

The protests have been some of the biggest and most powerful the world has ever seen, especially in the United States where tens of millions of people continue to come out to stand against racism and make sure that racial justice is at the centre of conversations about politics and culture. The protests have pushed local governments across the US to begin re-imagining their cities as places with fewer police and more investment in communities. Black Lives Matter is sounding the alarm that there is a long way to go for Black people to feel safe and respected. The work is not over.

Digital

Even before the invention of the internet, activists were using digital technologies to scramble and pass messages. As technology has continued to develop, so have the many ways in which people protest in virtual space.

SPAM THE SYSTEM, 1990s

When the British government were trying to control 1990s rave culture, they banned playing music with a repetitive beat at raves. In protest, the people who loved this music decided to disrupt the status quo in a new way. They began sending thousands of emails to UK politicians, jamming their inboxes and causing government websites to shut down for over a week. Methods like hashtag activism used today evolved from this tactic.

VIRTUAL SIT-IN, 1995

Italian organisation Strano Network were one of the first groups to use a tactic called a DoS – or denial of service attack – in this case against the French government's nuclear policy. In these 'virtual sit-ins', thousands of people visit a website at the same time and click the refresh button over and over again until the site crashes. Even though the technique is quite simple, it is still used today by groups like Anonymous, who also use more sophisticated hacking techniques to disrupt websites and release information to the public.

BLOGGING FOR FREEDOM, 2009

Malala Yousafzai grew up in an area of northwest Pakistan occupied by a terrorist group called the Taliban. They wanted to stop girls being educated, but Malala loved school and wanted to learn. When she was just 11, Malala began an anonymous blog for the BBC about daily life under the Taliban. She kept the blog for several years until it became so popular that eventually her identity was revealed, and even though she was just a child with a computer, the Taliban tried to kill her. She was flown to the UK where she recovered and started going to school again. At age 17 Malala was the youngest person ever to win the Nobel Peace Prize.

K-POP VS POTUS, 2020

When US President Donald Trump made plans for a huge election rally despite the coronavirus pandemic and Black Lives Matter protests, opposition came from a surprising source. Fans of K-pop (Korean pop music) used skills honed by buying concert tickets to reserve thousands of seats at the rally. But they never intended to use them. After bragging about how a million people wanted to hear him speak, Trump was embarrassed when he looked out over the enormous arena to see thousands of empty seats. K-pop fans also supported BLM by using their network to hijack the opposing "Blue Lives Matter" hashtag with memes of blue cartoon characters like the Smurfs, and to raise millions of dollars for the cause.

BEST SELFIE EVER, 2016

When trans woman Sarah McBride was travelling on business, she needed a pee. If she had been in her home state of Washington D.C. this wouldn't have been a problem – but now she was in North Carolina, where a new law meant that people could only use public toilets that matched the gender assigned to them at birth. Sarah walked right into the women's restroom and took a selfie. "We are all just people," she wrote. "Trying to pee in peace." The post received tens of thousands of shares, was featured on the news and raised awareness about how trans people were being treated in North Carolina. Within a year the law was overturned.

OPERATION VULA, 1980s

Because South African anti-apartheid activists were often spied on by the government, they needed a secret way to communicate. Tim Jenkin was a South African living in London, who had been trying to solve this problem for years. Eventually, his system was ready. Janet Love, an activist in Johannesburg, would type messages on a laptop and convert them into code, which would be converted into sound. Next, Janet phoned Tim and played the strange noise into his answering machine. In London, Tim converted the sound back into the original message, and passed that on to other exiled activists around the world.

Green shoots

New Grassroots

ZUZECA SAPA, THE BLACK SNAKE
Dakota Access Pipeline Protests, North America, 2016-

The ancestors of the Lakota, Dakota and Nakota tribes had a prophecy: one day a giant black snake would appear, winding its way across the land and putting Unci Maka, Grandmother Earth, in danger. For years people wondered when the black snake would come and what it would look like. Was it the new highways that snaked over the country? Then they heard of plans for a pipeline. It would carry thick black oil from deep within the earth of North Dakota for over a thousand miles across sacred Native lands. They knew this was it – Zuzeca Sapa, the black snake, had come.

The people knew that water was life, and that without clean water, humans and wildlife couldn't survive. The Dakota Access Pipeline threatened to pollute Mni Sose, the Missouri river. To the people, it wasn't just a river – it was part of their family. And just as you would protect a relative, they would protect the river.

The prophecy also foretold a story of resistance: when the black snake appeared the people would come together to cut off its head. And that is what happened.

At the very first meetings with the oil companies the Native People stood up and said they didn't want the pipeline. The land belonged to them, according to an old treaty from 1851. The elders began to protest with letters, speeches and petitions, and even started a small camp near one of the sacred sites that was due to be bulldozed, so they could keep an eye on what was happening.

Meanwhile, the young people protested in their own way. In relays, teenagers ran thousands of miles to deliver petitions. They even ran to the White House to see if the President would help. When they arrived, he didn't come out to see them – but all over the world, other people were watching. By the end of the summer people had come to join the small camp at Standing Rock in solidarity – so many that a new camp was set up to make room for them all.

The camp was a place of togetherness like the ones spoken about in old stories. At the heart of the camp was a fire that was kept burning day and night. Around the fire, people sang, danced, cooked and plotted. Everyone had a role, from chopping wood to running the camp school. The camp itself was a form of resistance against the colonisation that the white settlers had begun hundreds of years ago. It also taught skills for taking direct action – every day, marches and small groups left from the camp to go to the digging sites, where some chained themselves to the bulldozers and others distracted the police.

Despite the peacefulness of the camps, the government and the oil companies kept sending in police and soldiers. They tried to scare off the protesters with water cannons, dogs and tear gas.

Although it was very scary, the protesters stayed long enough to win support from the President, though they lost it from the next. Behind the scenes, the Water Protectors kept working. Although the pipeline carried oil for three years, the protesters did not stop telling the world that they have rights and that fuel companies need to switch to energy solutions that do not harm the natural world. At the time of writing, the pipeline has been shut down and oil has stopped flowing through the body of the black snake, while arguments about its future continue.

NO ACTION IS TOO RADICAL

Extinction Rebellion, Global, 2018-

XR is a **MASS CIVIL DISOBEDIENCE MOVEMENT** inspired by civil rights activists and the Suffragettes

This time, responding to the **CLIMATE CRISIS**

Tactics include stopping traffic, shutting down bridges and occupying public spaces

ACT NOW

SORRY FOR THE INCONVENIENCE!

CLIMATE

REBEL FOR LIFE

WAKE UP!

Thousands of ordinary people have allowed themselves to be arrested in order to change attitudes to climate change

and to spur governments into action!

Now there are **REBELS** in over 70 different countries

and **CLIMATE EMERGENCY** has been declared around the world

EMERGENCY

SCHOOL STRIKE

Fridays For Future, Global, 2018-

The weather was getting weirder, but no one wanted to talk about it. It was Sweden's hottest summer for 262 years and Greta Thunberg, a 15-year-old high school student, was worried. Everywhere she looked, politicians and grown-ups were pretending it wasn't a problem.

If they wouldn't take action, she would. One Monday morning, instead of going to school, she walked to the Swedish parliament building where politicians would see the message written on her sign as they came in and out of the building: SCHOOL STRIKE FOR CLIMATE. After sitting outside on the cobblestones all day, she posted a picture on social media and went home. The next day she got up and headed back to Parliament, ready to spend another day protesting alone. But before long she was joined by people who cared as much as she did. They'd seen her post, re-posted it, and by the end of the week, newspapers were there taking pictures.

The school-strikers stayed there every day until Sweden's next election. But even though the strikes had got people talking, the politicians were still wasting time. After the election the strikes continued every Friday, and Greta was invited all over Europe to give speeches which were watched by people everywhere. By March the next year 1.4 million school children were on strike in villages, towns and cities from New York to Nairobi.

The world is full of young people leading the fight for environmental justice.

Indigenous activist Autumn Peltier was 13 years old when she challenged Canadian Prime Minister Justin Trudeau on the oil pipeline being built on Indigenous land. She is now the Chief Water Commissioner for the Anishinabek Nation, protecting Native land and water.

When Vanessa Nakate heard about the global school strikes she wanted to start one where she lived in Uganda. Because protesting there can be dangerous, none of her friends wanted to strike, but her siblings joined her. Since then, she has led three national climate strikes, and battled racism in media coverage of climate activism.

Artemisa Xakriabá is a young Indigenous activist from Brazil who is passionate about rainforests. She has seen first-hand the effects of the fires in the Amazon, and works with The Guardians of the Forest, a group of Indigenous communities which protect over 400 million hectares of rainforest and its people.

In Guilin, China, youth activist Howey Ou has taken bold risks to protest for climate action – she has been expelled from school for striking, and has had to move away from home. After she was told to leave government offices where she was holding a lone protest, Howey started planting trees around the buildings, an initiative she calls Plant for Survival.

Elizabeth Wanjiru Wathuti from Kenya planted her first tree at 7 years old. By the time she was 21 she had founded the Green Generation Initiative, which has planted over 30,000 trees by working with schools and young people.

Isra Hirsi, the co-founder of US Youth Climate Strike, has been helping to create a climate movement in which activists of colour have a strong voice since she was 16. She speaks up about how people of colour are the most affected by the climate crisis.

Like Isra Hirsi, Zanagee Artis works to draw attention to the connections between racism, colonialism and the climate crisis through the youth organisation Zero Hour movement. Together they have organised youth climate summits, marches, lobby days and arts festivals.

Youth-led political group The Sunrise Movement held a 1000-person sit-in at politicians' offices in Washington D.C. to demand a Green New Deal. They work tirelessly to bring climate change into focus in political debate.

Indian climate activist Ridhima Pandey was 9 years old when she sued the Indian Government over inaction on climate change. Since then, she has joined Greta Thunberg and other youth activists from around the world in filing a complaint with the United Nations, accusing five countries of violating children's rights by ignoring the risks of climate change.

Solidarity

TACTICS

Throughout history, groups who are oppressed have understood that their struggles are connected. Acting in solidarity by standing side by side is a way to show support and share strength.

EVICTION BLOCKADES, 1930s

The Great Depression left millions in the USA without wages and at risk of losing their homes. People joined branches of the National Unemployment Council, and turned up together outside their friends' and neighbours' front doors, their act of solidarity preventing landlords from turfing families out. Eviction blockades are still used today as a way to keep tenants in their homes, like when 80 people from the group Take Back the Land surrounded a family home in Rochester, NY in 2011. The bailiffs gave up and went home.

LESBIANS AND GAYS SUPPORT THE MINERS, 1980s

Coal miners were on strike in the largest action by British workers for decades: the government was starting to shut down the industry without supporting mining communities. The LGBTQ+ community knew how it felt to have their needs overlooked. After collecting donations at that summer's Pride march, Lesbians and Gays Support the Miners was born. LGSM activists visited the miners, who were so moved that they vowed to help fight the discrimination LGBTQ+ people were facing in society and at work. At the next year's Pride, the National Union of Miners headed the march.

LESBIANS AND GAYS SUPPORT THE MIGRANTS, 2017

Inspired by LGSM's support of the mining community, Lesbians and Gays Support the Migrants protest the discrimination and human rights abuses that many migrants face. Aiming to stop the deportation of 60 migrants, 15 members of LGSM and End Deportations chained themselves in front of a plane heading for West Africa so it couldn't take off from the runway at Stansted Airport. Eleven of the migrants now have legal status in the UK. LGSM have kept making a noise for migrants' rights. In the words of one of their giant banners, "queer solidarity smashes borders".

CHAIN OF FREEDOM, 1989

When the countries along the Baltic Sea were trying to win independence from Soviet rule, millions of citizens held hands and linked arms across three countries – Estonia, Latvia and Lithuania. Together they made a human chain 600 km (370 miles) long. It was called the Baltic Way. People who were there say that by joining hands, they could sense the energy of all the other protesters, creating a feeling of togetherness, solidarity, and power. Within months, Lithuania announced its independence, and the other Baltic countries soon followed.

PROUD PARLIAMENT, 2020

Poland had just re-elected a President who openly opposed LGBTQ+ rights, and people were getting harassed and arrested just for displaying rainbow and trans flags. Left-wing members of parliament made a bold move to show their support for the country's queer community. On the day of President Duda's swearing-in, they coordinated their outfits so that when they stood next to each other, they created a rainbow. The EU also showed solidarity by denying funding for six towns declaring themselves 'LGBT-free zones'.

BATHROOM SIT-IN, 2016

When North Carolina passed a bill stripping civil rights from LGBTQ+ people, allowing businesses to discriminate against queer customers and forcing trans people to use the wrong toilets, the local NAACP stepped in. Having taken part in the civil rights movement, these Black activists knew that not only were trans African Americans put especially at risk by the new bill, but remembered the Jim Crow laws used to segregate Black people up until the 1960s. They wouldn't let the laws return to harm queer people: they organised a mass sit-in against the law they renamed the 'hate bill'. "Like we sit, this legislation needs to be sat down," said organiser Reverend William Barber.

WEDDING PROTECTORS, 2011

During the Arab Spring revolution in Egypt, many weddings were cancelled, as venues shut down in the unrest. But lots of couples decided that Tahrir Square at the centre of the protests in Cairo would make an even better place to get married, and would bring joy and optimism to the tired crowds. When one Christian couple tied the knot amid the tanks surrounding the square, Muslim protesters formed a ring around them, so the blessing could happen in peace. In turn, Christians gathered around Muslims while they prayed. The Square was united by the spirit of the revolution.

THANKS

We are indebted to many historians, researchers and writers.

Some of the most useful general books on protest movements we have used include *Beautiful Trouble* edited by Andrew Boyd and Dave Oswald Mitchell, and its sister book *Beautiful Rising* edited by Juman Abujbara, Andrew Boyd, Dave Oswald Mitchell, and Marcel Taminato; Steve Crawshaw's books *Street Spirit* and *Small Acts of Resistance* (with John Jackson); *Why Civil Resistance Works* by Erica Chenoweth and Maria Stephan; *This is an Uprising* by Mark Engler and Paul Engler; *How to Change the World* by John Paul Flintoff; *Disobedient Objects* by Catherine Flood and Gavin Grindon; *Direct Action* by LA Kauffman; *Nonviolence* by Mark Kurlansky; *Why It's Still Kicking Off Everywhere* by Paul Mason; *Fighting Sleep* by Franny Nudelman; *It Was Like a Fever* by Francesca Polletta; *Blueprint for Revolution* by Srdja Popovic; *Space Invaders* by Paul Routledge; *Hope in the Dark* by Rebecca Solnit; and the wonderful, classic encyclopedia of protest tactics, *The Politics of Nonviolent Action* by Gene Sharp.

Particular chapters could not have been written without the help of specific books, including *India's Ancient Past* by R. S. Sharma (the Kalabhra Revolt); *The World Turned Upside Down* by Christopher Hill (the Levellers and the Diggers); *Our History is The Future* by Nick Estes (the Ghost Dance and Dakota Access Pipeline resistance); *Abolition!* by Richard S. Reddie (Resistance to Slavery); Mark Kurlansky's books *Nonviolence* (Protest Ploughs and the Salt March) and *1968* (the May '68 student protests); *Non-Violence and the French Revolution* by Micah Alpaugh; *Riot!* by Ian Hernon (Peterloo); 'The History of May Day' by Eric Hobsbawm (an article in Tribune magazine); *The Suffragettes in Pictures* by Diane Atkinson (Votes for Women); *African Women, A Modern History* by Catherine Coquery-Vidrovitch (The Women Take Down the King); *Resistance and Revolution* by Sheila Rowbotham (Women Unite); *The Rebellious Life of Rosa Parks* by Jeanne Theoharis (Civil Rights); *Popular Protest in Palestine* by Marwan Darweish and Andrew Rigby; and the extremely in-depth and impressive children's books *Stonewall Riots* by Gayle E. Pitman and *Suffragette* by David Roberts.

We relied on the documentaries *The World Against Apartheid: Have You Heard from Johannesburg?* by Clarity Films; and the BBC documentaries *Greenham Common Changed my Life* and *Storyville: The People v. The Party* (Tiananmen Square).

We would also like to thank the People's History Museum in Manchester, UK, where we researched Peterloo and other UK-based movements; the National Center for Civil and Human Rights in Atlanta, and the Revolution 89 exhibition in Berlin (and also online at www.revolution89.de).

There are lots of excellent books on protest written for children, many of which inspired the chapters in this book. Some of these include: *Challenge Everything* by Blue Sandford; the *Little Leaders* series by Vashti Harrison; *Suffragette* by David Roberts; *Women in Battle* by Jenny Jordahl and Marta Breen; *Stonewall Riots: Coming out in the streets* by Gayle E. Pitman; *Kid Activists* by Robin Stevenson and Allison Steinfeld.

We have quoted from activists in the titles of some chapters. 'The old world is running up like parchment in the fire' – Gerrard Winstanley, Digger. 'Roll them up like a carpet' is a paraphrase of the full quote by Lakota leader Lame Deer which appears on page 42. 'Ye are many, they are few' – Percy Bysshe Shelley, in his poem 'The Masque of Anarchy', written about Peterloo. 'We're not ugly, we're not beautiful, we're angry' – slogan on a placard held by Women's Lib protesters outside the 1970 Miss World Contest. 'Truth Force' is a translation of Gandhi's concept of satyagraha. 'Until justice rolls down like waters' – Martin Luther King, Jr. 'Be realistic, demand the impossible' – slogan from the May '68 student protests. 'Freedom for those who think differently' – Rosa Luxembourg quote revived in the struggle to bring down the Berlin wall. 'Another world is possible' – slogan used at the Battle of Seattle. 'Be like water' – Bruce Lee, used as a slogan by Hong Kong pro-democracy protesters. 'Mubarak: Go! My arms are tired' (placard on page 144) – slogan seen at Tahrir Square, as reported by Paul Mason in *Why it's Kicking Off Everywhere*.

We would also like to extend our heartfelt thanks to the people who have made this book possible. Our brilliant editors, Neil Dunnicliffe, Hattie Grylls and Martha Owen for commissioning the book and editing it with such care and enthusiasm. Ian Bloom for lending his legal expertise and eagle eyes to the text. Sarah Crookes, Jess Arvidsson, Colette Whitehouse and Catherine Ward for their invaluable work on the design, production, marketing and publicity. Stellar agent Ed Wilson who makes even the paperwork fun. Rachel Stubbs who has generously coloured so many of the illustrations and done much of the hand-lettering including the beautiful banners and posters on the May '68, May Day and Votes for Women pages. Emily's students and all at the Royal Drawing School for their flexibility and support. Anouchka Grose, Mark Tittle, Connie Buchholz and Domino for keeping us healthy and sane. Jack Rattenbury for being an early reader of the book and making excellent suggestions on the text. Dax Rossetti for cooking and listening and telling us about Gino Bartali. Our friends, particularly Clémence Viel, Sophie Herxheimer, Sybille Pouzet, Gemma Curtis, Claire Lamont, Tamsin Omond, Kristin Bird, Shannon Burns, and Jenelle Stafford. Thank you to all the people we have protested with who have inspired us so much, and especially our parents who have encouraged us in every way. And thank you to the brave protesters whose stories have filled the pages of this book and who have never stopped working to make the world a better place.

"I used to think I had to wait to be an adult to lead.
But I've learned that even a child's voice can be heard around the world."

MALALA YOUSAFZAI